Free Gift!

Want a free gift?

Email us at
betterlifejournals@gmail.com

Title the email "Journal" and we will send you
something fun!

Visit our website for more:
https://lifelabmagazine.com/better-life-
journals/

More Journals!

Want a Journal to give your busy friend or family member as a gift, or just want more Journal ideas?

Check out some of our other Journals...

Your Weekly Self Care Checklist
Gratitude Leaf: Creative Gratitude Journal
Weekly Better Health Checklist
Your Weekly Mental Health Checklist
Your Weekly Happiness Checklist
The Wheel of Life Workbook
The Positivity Workbook
Your Weekly Self Improvement Checklist

Choose from different lengths (60 days, 90 days and more) as well as different types of journals (with different goals and objectives). You are sure to find something that'll be great both as a personal journal and as a gift!

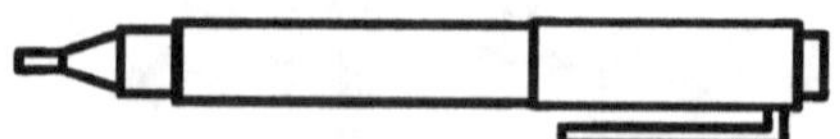

YOUR WEEKLY FIBROMYALGIA CARE CHECKLIST

To keep the
body in good
health is a duty.
otherwise we
shall not be able
to keep the
mind strong
and clear

BUDDHA

GETTING STARTED

The workbook and journal is pretty self-explanatory so you can just go through it at your own pace. That said, here are some tips that can help you get the most out of this:

- **Schedule a specific time** in the day when you will work on this workbook over the coming days. Having a specific time will help you stay on course. An easy way to do this is to schedule a recurring reminder on your phone's calendar.
- Start with the **Personal Assessment**.
- Next, work on the empowering **habit creator** section. This can help you create one good habit over the next 90 days, which will have a big impact on your wellbeing and happiness.
- Go through the **Wellbeing activities** list to get ideas for what you can do to take better care of yourself.
- Complete the journal pages every week (ideally daily) over the coming days. Take a bit of time before you get started to mentally prepare yourself if you need to but once you start, commit to doing them every day.

Most importantly, take it one day at a time. Small actions overtime will get you big results, as you will soon find out :)

Let's begin!

Good health is not something we can buy. However, it can be an extremely valuable savings account

ANNE WILSON SCHAEF

PERSONAL ASSESSMENT

1. What does looking after my health better mean to me?

2. What does me having better health look like?

3. Current level of health   1 2 3 4 5

4. Desired level of health   1 2 3 4 5

PERSONAL ASSESSMENT

5. Why is it important for me to improve my health?

6. Who is the most healthy I know, and what do I like most about them/their life?

7. What are the things I can do regularly to improve my health (both both big and small, like learning something new)?

DECLARATION

I hereby commit to this daily practice.

Sign:

Date:

It is health that is the real wealth, and not pieces of gold and silver

MAHATMA GANDHI

HEALTHY HABIT CREATOR

Pick one small thing you can do every day for the next 90 days, something that will benefit your health (e.g. meditation, exercise, gratitude log, etc).

Once you have decided, use the habit tracker below to stick to this small daily positive habit by ticking/coloring one box for every day you practice the habit.

ONE THING = ______________________________

To ensure good health: eat lightly, breathe deeply, live moderately, cultivate cheerfulness, and maintain an interest in life

WILLIAM LONDEN

WELLBEING ACTIVITIES

Make a list of things that make you feel happy/good (we've included some ideas to get you started).

This list will come in very handy when planning your daily activities, and especially on days you aren't feeling so good (we all have off days, so it's ok).

- ◯ Workout (even a 3-5 minutes of physical exercise can have a positive impact on your mood, and wellbeing)

- ◯ Practice gratitude (practicing gratitude can not only help you feel good in the short term, but in the long term too!)

- ◯ Meditation (practicing meditation can help you to regulate your emotions, and stress, better)

- ◯ Random acts of kindness (being nice & helping others is one of the best ways, if not the best way, to feel joy)

- ◯ Enjoy a nice cup of your favorite tea or coffee (even small things like this can have a big impact on your mood)

- ◯

- ◯

WELLBEING
ACTIVITIES

In order to be the
master of your life,
you must first
recognize that you
are the rightful
master of your
brain, its owner
and operator

ILCHI LEE

START YOUR JOURNEY!

EAT CLEAN & EXERCISE
STAY
HEALTHY

MY PRIORITIES FOR THIS WEEK

GRATITUDE LOG

MAIN GOALS

DAILY ACTIVITIES

	M	T	W	T	F	S	S
Meditate	○	○	○	○	○	○	○
Exercise	○	○	○	○	○	○	○
Gratitude log	○	○	○	○	○	○	○
Sleep 7+ hours	○	○	○	○	○	○	○
Connect with others	○	○	○	○	○	○	○
Avoid alcohol	○	○	○	○	○	○	○
Less meat	○	○	○	○	○	○	○
Less dairy	○	○	○	○	○	○	○
Less refined carbs	○	○	○	○	○	○	○
Keep notes of triggers	○	○	○	○	○	○	○
Take Vitamin B12	○	○	○	○	○	○	○
Take Vitamin D	○	○	○	○	○	○	○

MY PRIORITIES FOR THIS WEEK

GRATITUDE LOG

MAIN GOALS

DAILY ACTIVITIES

	M	T	W	T	F	S	S
Meditate	○	○	○	○	○	○	○
Exercise	○	○	○	○	○	○	○
Gratitude log	○	○	○	○	○	○	○
Sleep 7+ hours	○	○	○	○	○	○	○
Connect with others	○	○	○	○	○	○	○
Avoid alcohol	○	○	○	○	○	○	○
Less meat	○	○	○	○	○	○	○
Less dairy	○	○	○	○	○	○	○
Less refined carbs	○	○	○	○	○	○	○
Keep notes of triggers	○	○	○	○	○	○	○
Take Vitamin B12	○	○	○	○	○	○	○
Take Vitamin D	○	○	○	○	○	○	○

MY PRIORITIES FOR THIS WEEK

GRATITUDE LOG

MAIN GOALS

DAILY ACTIVITIES

	M	T	W	T	F	S	S
Meditate	○	○	○	○	○	○	○
Exercise	○	○	○	○	○	○	○
Gratitude log	○	○	○	○	○	○	○
Sleep 7+ hours	○	○	○	○	○	○	○
Connect with others	○	○	○	○	○	○	○
Avoid alcohol	○	○	○	○	○	○	○
Less meat	○	○	○	○	○	○	○
Less dairy	○	○	○	○	○	○	○
Less refined carbs	○	○	○	○	○	○	○
Keep notes of triggers	○	○	○	○	○	○	○
Take Vitamin B12	○	○	○	○	○	○	○
Take Vitamin D	○	○	○	○	○	○	○

WEEK OF:

MY PRIORITIES FOR THIS WEEK

GRATITUDE LOG

MAIN GOALS

DAILY ACTIVITIES

M T W T F S S

Meditate
Exercise
Gratitude log
Sleep 7+ hours
Connect with others
Avoid alcohol
Less meat
Less dairy
Less refined carbs
Keep notes of
triggers
Take Vitamin B12
Take Vitamin D

MY PRIORITIES FOR THIS WEEK

GRATITUDE LOG

MAIN GOALS

DAILY ACTIVITIES

	M	T	W	T	F	S	S
Meditate	○	○	○	○	○	○	○
Exercise	○	○	○	○	○	○	○
Gratitude log	○	○	○	○	○	○	○
Sleep 7+ hours	○	○	○	○	○	○	○
Connect with others	○	○	○	○	○	○	○
Avoid alcohol	○	○	○	○	○	○	○
Less meat	○	○	○	○	○	○	○
Less dairy	○	○	○	○	○	○	○
Less refined carbs	○	○	○	○	○	○	○
Keep notes of triggers	○	○	○	○	○	○	○
Take Vitamin B12	○	○	○	○	○	○	○
Take Vitamin D	○	○	○	○	○	○	○

MY PRIORITIES FOR THIS WEEK

GRATITUDE LOG

MAIN GOALS

DAILY ACTIVITIES

	M	T	W	T	F	S	S
Meditate	○	○	○	○	○	○	○
Exercise	○	○	○	○	○	○	○
Gratitude log	○	○	○	○	○	○	○
Sleep 7+ hours	○	○	○	○	○	○	○
Connect with others	○	○	○	○	○	○	○
Avoid alcohol	○	○	○	○	○	○	○
Less meat	○	○	○	○	○	○	○
Less dairy	○	○	○	○	○	○	○
Less refined carbs	○	○	○	○	○	○	○
Keep notes of triggers	○	○	○	○	○	○	○
Take Vitamin B12	○	○	○	○	○	○	○
Take Vitamin D	○	○	○	○	○	○	○

MY PRIORITIES FOR THIS WEEK

GRATITUDE LOG

MAIN GOALS

DAILY ACTIVITIES

	M	T	W	T	F	S	S
Meditate	○	○	○	○	○	○	○
Exercise	○	○	○	○	○	○	○
Gratitude log	○	○	○	○	○	○	○
Sleep 7+ hours	○	○	○	○	○	○	○
Connect with others	○	○	○	○	○	○	○
Avoid alcohol	○	○	○	○	○	○	○
Less meat	○	○	○	○	○	○	○
Less dairy	○	○	○	○	○	○	○
Less refined carbs	○	○	○	○	○	○	○
Keep notes of triggers	○	○	○	○	○	○	○
Take Vitamin B12	○	○	○	○	○	○	○
Take Vitamin D	○	○	○	○	○	○	○

MY PRIORITIES FOR THIS WEEK

GRATITUDE LOG

MAIN GOALS

DAILY ACTIVITIES

	M	T	W	T	F	S	S
Meditate	○	○	○	○	○	○	○
Exercise	○	○	○	○	○	○	○
Gratitude log	○	○	○	○	○	○	○
Sleep 7+ hours	○	○	○	○	○	○	○
Connect with others	○	○	○	○	○	○	○
Avoid alcohol	○	○	○	○	○	○	○
Less meat	○	○	○	○	○	○	○
Less dairy	○	○	○	○	○	○	○
Less refined carbs	○	○	○	○	○	○	○
Keep notes of triggers	○	○	○	○	○	○	○
Take Vitamin B12	○	○	○	○	○	○	○
Take Vitamin D	○	○	○	○	○	○	○

MY PRIORITIES FOR THIS WEEK

GRATITUDE LOG

MAIN GOALS

DAILY ACTIVITIES

	M	T	W	T	F	S	S
Meditate	○	○	○	○	○	○	○
Exercise	○	○	○	○	○	○	○
Gratitude log	○	○	○	○	○	○	○
Sleep 7+ hours	○	○	○	○	○	○	○
Connect with others	○	○	○	○	○	○	○
Avoid alcohol	○	○	○	○	○	○	○
Less meat	○	○	○	○	○	○	○
Less dairy	○	○	○	○	○	○	○
Less refined carbs	○	○	○	○	○	○	○
Keep notes of triggers	○	○	○	○	○	○	○
Take Vitamin B12	○	○	○	○	○	○	○
Take Vitamin D	○	○	○	○	○	○	○

MY PRIORITIES FOR THIS WEEK

GRATITUDE LOG

MAIN GOALS

DAILY ACTIVITIES

	M	T	W	T	F	S	S
Meditate	○	○	○	○	○	○	○
Exercise	○	○	○	○	○	○	○
Gratitude log	○	○	○	○	○	○	○
Sleep 7+ hours	○	○	○	○	○	○	○
Connect with others	○	○	○	○	○	○	○
Avoid alcohol	○	○	○	○	○	○	○
Less meat	○	○	○	○	○	○	○
Less dairy	○	○	○	○	○	○	○
Less refined carbs	○	○	○	○	○	○	○
Keep notes of triggers	○	○	○	○	○	○	○
Take Vitamin B12	○	○	○	○	○	○	○
Take Vitamin D	○	○	○	○	○	○	○

MY PRIORITIES FOR THIS WEEK

GRATITUDE LOG

MAIN GOALS

DAILY ACTIVITIES

	M	T	W	T	F	S	S
Meditate	○	○	○	○	○	○	○
Exercise	○	○	○	○	○	○	○
Gratitude log	○	○	○	○	○	○	○
Sleep 7+ hours	○	○	○	○	○	○	○
Connect with others	○	○	○	○	○	○	○
Avoid alcohol	○	○	○	○	○	○	○
Less meat	○	○	○	○	○	○	○
Less dairy	○	○	○	○	○	○	○
Less refined carbs	○	○	○	○	○	○	○
Keep notes of triggers	○	○	○	○	○	○	○
Take Vitamin B12	○	○	○	○	○	○	○
Take Vitamin D	○	○	○	○	○	○	○

MY PRIORITIES FOR THIS WEEK

GRATITUDE LOG

MAIN GOALS

DAILY ACTIVITIES

	M	T	W	T	F	S	S
Meditate	○	○	○	○	○	○	○
Exercise	○	○	○	○	○	○	○
Gratitude log	○	○	○	○	○	○	○
Sleep 7+ hours	○	○	○	○	○	○	○
Connect with others	○	○	○	○	○	○	○
Avoid alcohol	○	○	○	○	○	○	○
Less meat	○	○	○	○	○	○	○
Less dairy	○	○	○	○	○	○	○
Less refined carbs	○	○	○	○	○	○	○
Keep notes of triggers	○	○	○	○	○	○	○
Take Vitamin B12	○	○	○	○	○	○	○
Take Vitamin D	○	○	○	○	○	○	○

MY PRIORITIES FOR THIS WEEK

GRATITUDE LOG

MAIN GOALS

DAILY ACTIVITIES

	M	T	W	T	F	S	S
Meditate	○	○	○	○	○	○	○
Exercise	○	○	○	○	○	○	○
Gratitude log	○	○	○	○	○	○	○
Sleep 7+ hours	○	○	○	○	○	○	○
Connect with others	○	○	○	○	○	○	○
Avoid alcohol	○	○	○	○	○	○	○
Less meat	○	○	○	○	○	○	○
Less dairy	○	○	○	○	○	○	○
Less refined carbs	○	○	○	○	○	○	○
Keep notes of triggers	○	○	○	○	○	○	○
Take Vitamin B12	○	○	○	○	○	○	○
Take Vitamin D	○	○	○	○	○	○	○

MY PRIORITIES FOR THIS WEEK

GRATITUDE LOG

MAIN GOALS

DAILY ACTIVITIES

	M	T	W	T	F	S	S
Meditate	○	○	○	○	○	○	○
Exercise	○	○	○	○	○	○	○
Gratitude log	○	○	○	○	○	○	○
Sleep 7+ hours	○	○	○	○	○	○	○
Connect with others	○	○	○	○	○	○	○
Avoid alcohol	○	○	○	○	○	○	○
Less meat	○	○	○	○	○	○	○
Less dairy	○	○	○	○	○	○	○
Less refined carbs	○	○	○	○	○	○	○
Keep notes of triggers	○	○	○	○	○	○	○
Take Vitamin B12	○	○	○	○	○	○	○
Take Vitamin D	○	○	○	○	○	○	○

MY PRIORITIES FOR THIS WEEK

GRATITUDE LOG

MAIN GOALS

DAILY ACTIVITIES

	M	T	W	T	F	S	S
Meditate	○	○	○	○	○	○	○
Exercise	○	○	○	○	○	○	○
Gratitude log	○	○	○	○	○	○	○
Sleep 7+ hours	○	○	○	○	○	○	○
Connect with others	○	○	○	○	○	○	○
Avoid alcohol	○	○	○	○	○	○	○
Less meat	○	○	○	○	○	○	○
Less dairy	○	○	○	○	○	○	○
Less refined carbs	○	○	○	○	○	○	○
Keep notes of triggers	○	○	○	○	○	○	○
Take Vitamin B12	○	○	○	○	○	○	○
Take Vitamin D	○	○	○	○	○	○	○

MY PRIORITIES FOR THIS WEEK

GRATITUDE LOG

MAIN GOALS

DAILY ACTIVITIES

	M	T	W	T	F	S	S
Meditate	○	○	○	○	○	○	○
Exercise	○	○	○	○	○	○	○
Gratitude log	○	○	○	○	○	○	○
Sleep 7+ hours	○	○	○	○	○	○	○
Connect with others	○	○	○	○	○	○	○
Avoid alcohol	○	○	○	○	○	○	○
Less meat	○	○	○	○	○	○	○
Less dairy	○	○	○	○	○	○	○
Less refined carbs	○	○	○	○	○	○	○
Keep notes of triggers	○	○	○	○	○	○	○
Take Vitamin B12	○	○	○	○	○	○	○
Take Vitamin D	○	○	○	○	○	○	○

MY PRIORITIES FOR THIS WEEK

GRATITUDE LOG

MAIN GOALS

DAILY ACTIVITIES

	M	T	W	T	F	S	S
Meditate	○	○	○	○	○	○	○
Exercise	○	○	○	○	○	○	○
Gratitude log	○	○	○	○	○	○	○
Sleep 7+ hours	○	○	○	○	○	○	○
Connect with others	○	○	○	○	○	○	○
Avoid alcohol	○	○	○	○	○	○	○
Less meat	○	○	○	○	○	○	○
Less dairy	○	○	○	○	○	○	○
Less refined carbs	○	○	○	○	○	○	○
Keep notes of triggers	○	○	○	○	○	○	○
Take Vitamin B12	○	○	○	○	○	○	○
Take Vitamin D	○	○	○	○	○	○	○

MY PRIORITIES FOR THIS WEEK

GRATITUDE LOG

MAIN GOALS

DAILY ACTIVITIES

	M	T	W	T	F	S	S
Meditate	○	○	○	○	○	○	○
Exercise	○	○	○	○	○	○	○
Gratitude log	○	○	○	○	○	○	○
Sleep 7+ hours	○	○	○	○	○	○	○
Connect with others	○	○	○	○	○	○	○
Avoid alcohol	○	○	○	○	○	○	○
Less meat	○	○	○	○	○	○	○
Less dairy	○	○	○	○	○	○	○
Less refined carbs	○	○	○	○	○	○	○
Keep notes of triggers	○	○	○	○	○	○	○
Take Vitamin B12	○	○	○	○	○	○	○
Take Vitamin D	○	○	○	○	○	○	○

WEEK OF:

MY PRIORITIES FOR THIS WEEK

GRATITUDE LOG

MAIN GOALS

DAILY ACTIVITIES

M T W T F S S

Meditate
Exercise
Gratitude log
Sleep 7+ hours
Connect with others
Avoid alcohol
Less meat
Less dairy
Less refined carbs
Keep notes of triggers
Take Vitamin B12
Take Vitamin D

MY PRIORITIES FOR THIS WEEK

GRATITUDE LOG

MAIN GOALS

DAILY ACTIVITIES

	M	T	W	T	F	S	S
Meditate	○	○	○	○	○	○	○
Exercise	○	○	○	○	○	○	○
Gratitude log	○	○	○	○	○	○	○
Sleep 7+ hours	○	○	○	○	○	○	○
Connect with others	○	○	○	○	○	○	○
Avoid alcohol	○	○	○	○	○	○	○
Less meat	○	○	○	○	○	○	○
Less dairy	○	○	○	○	○	○	○
Less refined carbs	○	○	○	○	○	○	○
Keep notes of triggers	○	○	○	○	○	○	○
Take Vitamin B12	○	○	○	○	○	○	○
Take Vitamin D	○	○	○	○	○	○	○

MY PRIORITIES FOR THIS WEEK

GRATITUDE LOG

MAIN GOALS

DAILY ACTIVITIES

	M	T	W	T	F	S	S
Meditate	○	○	○	○	○	○	○
Exercise	○	○	○	○	○	○	○
Gratitude log	○	○	○	○	○	○	○
Sleep 7+ hours	○	○	○	○	○	○	○
Connect with others	○	○	○	○	○	○	○
Avoid alcohol	○	○	○	○	○	○	○
Less meat	○	○	○	○	○	○	○
Less dairy	○	○	○	○	○	○	○
Less refined carbs	○	○	○	○	○	○	○
Keep notes of triggers	○	○	○	○	○	○	○
Take Vitamin B12	○	○	○	○	○	○	○
Take Vitamin D	○	○	○	○	○	○	○

MY PRIORITIES FOR THIS WEEK

GRATITUDE LOG

MAIN GOALS

DAILY ACTIVITIES

	M	T	W	T	F	S	S
Meditate	○	○	○	○	○	○	○
Exercise	○	○	○	○	○	○	○
Gratitude log	○	○	○	○	○	○	○
Sleep 7+ hours	○	○	○	○	○	○	○
Connect with others	○	○	○	○	○	○	○
Avoid alcohol	○	○	○	○	○	○	○
Less meat	○	○	○	○	○	○	○
Less dairy	○	○	○	○	○	○	○
Less refined carbs	○	○	○	○	○	○	○
Keep notes of triggers	○	○	○	○	○	○	○
Take Vitamin B12	○	○	○	○	○	○	○
Take Vitamin D	○	○	○	○	○	○	○

MY PRIORITIES FOR THIS WEEK

GRATITUDE LOG

MAIN GOALS

DAILY ACTIVITIES

	M	T	W	T	F	S	S
Meditate	○	○	○	○	○	○	○
Exercise	○	○	○	○	○	○	○
Gratitude log	○	○	○	○	○	○	○
Sleep 7+ hours	○	○	○	○	○	○	○
Connect with others	○	○	○	○	○	○	○
Avoid alcohol	○	○	○	○	○	○	○
Less meat	○	○	○	○	○	○	○
Less dairy	○	○	○	○	○	○	○
Less refined carbs	○	○	○	○	○	○	○
Keep notes of triggers	○	○	○	○	○	○	○
Take Vitamin B12	○	○	○	○	○	○	○
Take Vitamin D	○	○	○	○	○	○	○

MY PRIORITIES FOR THIS WEEK

GRATITUDE LOG

MAIN GOALS

DAILY ACTIVITIES

	M	T	W	T	F	S	S
Meditate	○	○	○	○	○	○	○
Exercise	○	○	○	○	○	○	○
Gratitude log	○	○	○	○	○	○	○
Sleep 7+ hours	○	○	○	○	○	○	○
Connect with others	○	○	○	○	○	○	○
Avoid alcohol	○	○	○	○	○	○	○
Less meat	○	○	○	○	○	○	○
Less dairy	○	○	○	○	○	○	○
Less refined carbs	○	○	○	○	○	○	○
Keep notes of triggers	○	○	○	○	○	○	○
Take Vitamin B12	○	○	○	○	○	○	○
Take Vitamin D	○	○	○	○	○	○	○

MY PRIORITIES FOR THIS WEEK

GRATITUDE LOG

MAIN GOALS

DAILY ACTIVITIES

	M	T	W	T	F	S	S
Meditate	○	○	○	○	○	○	○
Exercise	○	○	○	○	○	○	○
Gratitude log	○	○	○	○	○	○	○
Sleep 7+ hours	○	○	○	○	○	○	○
Connect with others	○	○	○	○	○	○	○
Avoid alcohol	○	○	○	○	○	○	○
Less meat	○	○	○	○	○	○	○
Less dairy	○	○	○	○	○	○	○
Less refined carbs	○	○	○	○	○	○	○
Keep notes of triggers	○	○	○	○	○	○	○
Take Vitamin B12	○	○	○	○	○	○	○
Take Vitamin D	○	○	○	○	○	○	○

WEEK OF:

MY PRIORITIES FOR THIS WEEK

GRATITUDE LOG

MAIN GOALS

DAILY ACTIVITIES

M T W T F S S

Meditate
Exercise
Gratitude log
Sleep 7+ hours
Connect with others
Avoid alcohol
Less meat
Less dairy
Less refined carbs
Keep notes of triggers
Take Vitamin B12
Take Vitamin D

MY PRIORITIES FOR THIS WEEK

GRATITUDE LOG

MAIN GOALS

DAILY ACTIVITIES

	M	T	W	T	F	S	S
Meditate	○	○	○	○	○	○	○
Exercise	○	○	○	○	○	○	○
Gratitude log	○	○	○	○	○	○	○
Sleep 7+ hours	○	○	○	○	○	○	○
Connect with others	○	○	○	○	○	○	○
Avoid alcohol	○	○	○	○	○	○	○
Less meat	○	○	○	○	○	○	○
Less dairy	○	○	○	○	○	○	○
Less refined carbs	○	○	○	○	○	○	○
Keep notes of triggers	○	○	○	○	○	○	○
Take Vitamin B12	○	○	○	○	○	○	○
Take Vitamin D	○	○	○	○	○	○	○

MY PRIORITIES FOR THIS WEEK

GRATITUDE LOG

MAIN GOALS

DAILY ACTIVITIES

	M	T	W	T	F	S	S
Meditate	○	○	○	○	○	○	○
Exercise	○	○	○	○	○	○	○
Gratitude log	○	○	○	○	○	○	○
Sleep 7+ hours	○	○	○	○	○	○	○
Connect with others	○	○	○	○	○	○	○
Avoid alcohol	○	○	○	○	○	○	○
Less meat	○	○	○	○	○	○	○
Less dairy	○	○	○	○	○	○	○
Less refined carbs	○	○	○	○	○	○	○
Keep notes of triggers	○	○	○	○	○	○	○
Take Vitamin B12	○	○	○	○	○	○	○
Take Vitamin D	○	○	○	○	○	○	○

WEEK OF:

MY PRIORITIES FOR THIS WEEK

GRATITUDE LOG

MAIN GOALS

DAILY ACTIVITIES

M T W T F S S

Meditate
Exercise
Gratitude log
Sleep 7+ hours
Connect with others
Avoid alcohol
Less meat
Less dairy
Less refined carbs
Keep notes of triggers
Take Vitamin B12
Take Vitamin D

MY PRIORITIES FOR THIS WEEK

GRATITUDE LOG

MAIN GOALS

DAILY ACTIVITIES

	M	T	W	T	F	S	S
Meditate	○	○	○	○	○	○	○
Exercise	○	○	○	○	○	○	○
Gratitude log	○	○	○	○	○	○	○
Sleep 7+ hours	○	○	○	○	○	○	○
Connect with others	○	○	○	○	○	○	○
Avoid alcohol	○	○	○	○	○	○	○
Less meat	○	○	○	○	○	○	○
Less dairy	○	○	○	○	○	○	○
Less refined carbs	○	○	○	○	○	○	○
Keep notes of triggers	○	○	○	○	○	○	○
Take Vitamin B12	○	○	○	○	○	○	○
Take Vitamin D	○	○	○	○	○	○	○

MY PRIORITIES FOR THIS WEEK

GRATITUDE LOG

MAIN GOALS

DAILY ACTIVITIES

	M	T	W	T	F	S	S
Meditate	○	○	○	○	○	○	○
Exercise	○	○	○	○	○	○	○
Gratitude log	○	○	○	○	○	○	○
Sleep 7+ hours	○	○	○	○	○	○	○
Connect with others	○	○	○	○	○	○	○
Avoid alcohol	○	○	○	○	○	○	○
Less meat	○	○	○	○	○	○	○
Less dairy	○	○	○	○	○	○	○
Less refined carbs	○	○	○	○	○	○	○
Keep notes of triggers	○	○	○	○	○	○	○
Take Vitamin B12	○	○	○	○	○	○	○
Take Vitamin D	○	○	○	○	○	○	○

MY PRIORITIES FOR THIS WEEK

GRATITUDE LOG

MAIN GOALS

DAILY ACTIVITIES

	M	T	W	T	F	S	S
Meditate	○	○	○	○	○	○	○
Exercise	○	○	○	○	○	○	○
Gratitude log	○	○	○	○	○	○	○
Sleep 7+ hours	○	○	○	○	○	○	○
Connect with others	○	○	○	○	○	○	○
Avoid alcohol	○	○	○	○	○	○	○
Less meat	○	○	○	○	○	○	○
Less dairy	○	○	○	○	○	○	○
Less refined carbs	○	○	○	○	○	○	○
Keep notes of triggers	○	○	○	○	○	○	○
Take Vitamin B12	○	○	○	○	○	○	○
Take Vitamin D	○	○	○	○	○	○	○

WEEK OF:

MY PRIORITIES FOR THIS WEEK

GRATITUDE LOG

MAIN GOALS

DAILY ACTIVITIES

M T W T F S S

Meditate
Exercise
Gratitude log
Sleep 7+ hours
Connect with others
Avoid alcohol
Less meat
Less dairy
Less refined carbs
Keep notes of
triggers
Take Vitamin B12
Take Vitamin D

MY PRIORITIES FOR THIS WEEK

GRATITUDE LOG

MAIN GOALS

DAILY ACTIVITIES

	M	T	W	T	F	S	S
Meditate	○	○	○	○	○	○	○
Exercise	○	○	○	○	○	○	○
Gratitude log	○	○	○	○	○	○	○
Sleep 7+ hours	○	○	○	○	○	○	○
Connect with others	○	○	○	○	○	○	○
Avoid alcohol	○	○	○	○	○	○	○
Less meat	○	○	○	○	○	○	○
Less dairy	○	○	○	○	○	○	○
Less refined carbs	○	○	○	○	○	○	○
Keep notes of triggers	○	○	○	○	○	○	○
Take Vitamin B12	○	○	○	○	○	○	○
Take Vitamin D	○	○	○	○	○	○	○

MY PRIORITIES FOR THIS WEEK

GRATITUDE LOG

MAIN GOALS

DAILY ACTIVITIES

	M	T	W	T	F	S	S
Meditate	○	○	○	○	○	○	○
Exercise	○	○	○	○	○	○	○
Gratitude log	○	○	○	○	○	○	○
Sleep 7+ hours	○	○	○	○	○	○	○
Connect with others	○	○	○	○	○	○	○
Avoid alcohol	○	○	○	○	○	○	○
Less meat	○	○	○	○	○	○	○
Less dairy	○	○	○	○	○	○	○
Less refined carbs	○	○	○	○	○	○	○
Keep notes of triggers	○	○	○	○	○	○	○
Take Vitamin B12	○	○	○	○	○	○	○
Take Vitamin D	○	○	○	○	○	○	○

MY PRIORITIES FOR THIS WEEK

GRATITUDE LOG

MAIN GOALS

DAILY ACTIVITIES

	M	T	W	T	F	S	S
Meditate	○	○	○	○	○	○	○
Exercise	○	○	○	○	○	○	○
Gratitude log	○	○	○	○	○	○	○
Sleep 7+ hours	○	○	○	○	○	○	○
Connect with others	○	○	○	○	○	○	○
Avoid alcohol	○	○	○	○	○	○	○
Less meat	○	○	○	○	○	○	○
Less dairy	○	○	○	○	○	○	○
Less refined carbs	○	○	○	○	○	○	○
Keep notes of triggers	○	○	○	○	○	○	○
Take Vitamin B12	○	○	○	○	○	○	○
Take Vitamin D	○	○	○	○	○	○	○

WEEK OF:

MY PRIORITIES FOR THIS WEEK

GRATITUDE LOG

MAIN GOALS

DAILY ACTIVITIES

	M	T	W	T	F	S	S
Meditate	○	○	○	○	○	○	○
Exercise	○	○	○	○	○	○	○
Gratitude log	○	○	○	○	○	○	○
Sleep 7+ hours	○	○	○	○	○	○	○
Connect with others	○	○	○	○	○	○	○
Avoid alcohol	○	○	○	○	○	○	○
Less meat	○	○	○	○	○	○	○
Less dairy	○	○	○	○	○	○	○
Less refined carbs	○	○	○	○	○	○	○
Keep notes of triggers	○	○	○	○	○	○	○
Take Vitamin B12	○	○	○	○	○	○	○
Take Vitamin D	○	○	○	○	○	○	○

MY PRIORITIES FOR THIS WEEK

GRATITUDE LOG

MAIN GOALS

DAILY ACTIVITIES

	M	T	W	T	F	S	S
Meditate	◯	◯	◯	◯	◯	◯	◯
Exercise	◯	◯	◯	◯	◯	◯	◯
Gratitude log	◯	◯	◯	◯	◯	◯	◯
Sleep 7+ hours	◯	◯	◯	◯	◯	◯	◯
Connect with others	◯	◯	◯	◯	◯	◯	◯
Avoid alcohol	◯	◯	◯	◯	◯	◯	◯
Less meat	◯	◯	◯	◯	◯	◯	◯
Less dairy	◯	◯	◯	◯	◯	◯	◯
Less refined carbs	◯	◯	◯	◯	◯	◯	◯
Keep notes of triggers	◯	◯	◯	◯	◯	◯	◯
Take Vitamin B12	◯	◯	◯	◯	◯	◯	◯
Take Vitamin D	◯	◯	◯	◯	◯	◯	◯

MY PRIORITIES FOR THIS WEEK

GRATITUDE LOG

MAIN GOALS

DAILY ACTIVITIES

	M	T	W	T	F	S	S
Meditate	○	○	○	○	○	○	○
Exercise	○	○	○	○	○	○	○
Gratitude log	○	○	○	○	○	○	○
Sleep 7+ hours	○	○	○	○	○	○	○
Connect with others	○	○	○	○	○	○	○
Avoid alcohol	○	○	○	○	○	○	○
Less meat	○	○	○	○	○	○	○
Less dairy	○	○	○	○	○	○	○
Less refined carbs	○	○	○	○	○	○	○
Keep notes of triggers	○	○	○	○	○	○	○
Take Vitamin B12	○	○	○	○	○	○	○
Take Vitamin D	○	○	○	○	○	○	○

MY PRIORITIES FOR THIS WEEK

GRATITUDE LOG

MAIN GOALS

DAILY ACTIVITIES

	M	T	W	T	F	S	S
Meditate							
Exercise							
Gratitude log							
Sleep 7+ hours							
Connect with others							
Avoid alcohol							
Less meat							
Less dairy							
Less refined carbs							
Keep notes of triggers							
Take Vitamin B12							
Take Vitamin D							

MY PRIORITIES FOR THIS WEEK

GRATITUDE LOG

MAIN GOALS

DAILY ACTIVITIES

	M	T	W	T	F	S	S
Meditate	○	○	○	○	○	○	○
Exercise	○	○	○	○	○	○	○
Gratitude log	○	○	○	○	○	○	○
Sleep 7+ hours	○	○	○	○	○	○	○
Connect with others	○	○	○	○	○	○	○
Avoid alcohol	○	○	○	○	○	○	○
Less meat	○	○	○	○	○	○	○
Less dairy	○	○	○	○	○	○	○
Less refined carbs	○	○	○	○	○	○	○
Keep notes of triggers	○	○	○	○	○	○	○
Take Vitamin B12	○	○	○	○	○	○	○
Take Vitamin D	○	○	○	○	○	○	○

MY PRIORITIES FOR THIS WEEK

GRATITUDE LOG

MAIN GOALS

DAILY ACTIVITIES

	M	T	W	T	F	S	S
Meditate	○	○	○	○	○	○	○
Exercise	○	○	○	○	○	○	○
Gratitude log	○	○	○	○	○	○	○
Sleep 7+ hours	○	○	○	○	○	○	○
Connect with others	○	○	○	○	○	○	○
Avoid alcohol	○	○	○	○	○	○	○
Less meat	○	○	○	○	○	○	○
Less dairy	○	○	○	○	○	○	○
Less refined carbs	○	○	○	○	○	○	○
Keep notes of triggers	○	○	○	○	○	○	○
Take Vitamin B12	○	○	○	○	○	○	○
Take Vitamin D	○	○	○	○	○	○	○

MY PRIORITIES FOR THIS WEEK

GRATITUDE LOG

MAIN GOALS

DAILY ACTIVITIES

	M	T	W	T	F	S	S
Meditate	○	○	○	○	○	○	○
Exercise	○	○	○	○	○	○	○
Gratitude log	○	○	○	○	○	○	○
Sleep 7+ hours	○	○	○	○	○	○	○
Connect with others	○	○	○	○	○	○	○
Avoid alcohol	○	○	○	○	○	○	○
Less meat	○	○	○	○	○	○	○
Less dairy	○	○	○	○	○	○	○
Less refined carbs	○	○	○	○	○	○	○
Keep notes of triggers	○	○	○	○	○	○	○
Take Vitamin B12	○	○	○	○	○	○	○
Take Vitamin D	○	○	○	○	○	○	○

WEEK OF:

MY PRIORITIES FOR THIS WEEK

GRATITUDE LOG

MAIN GOALS

DAILY ACTIVITIES

M T W T F S S

Meditate
Exercise
Gratitude log
Sleep 7+ hours
Connect with others
Avoid alcohol
Less meat
Less dairy
Less refined carbs
Keep notes of triggers
Take Vitamin B12
Take Vitamin D

MY PRIORITIES FOR THIS WEEK

GRATITUDE LOG

MAIN GOALS

DAILY ACTIVITIES

	M	T	W	T	F	S	S
Meditate	◯	◯	◯	◯	◯	◯	◯
Exercise	◯	◯	◯	◯	◯	◯	◯
Gratitude log	◯	◯	◯	◯	◯	◯	◯
Sleep 7+ hours	◯	◯	◯	◯	◯	◯	◯
Connect with others	◯	◯	◯	◯	◯	◯	◯
Avoid alcohol	◯	◯	◯	◯	◯	◯	◯
Less meat	◯	◯	◯	◯	◯	◯	◯
Less dairy	◯	◯	◯	◯	◯	◯	◯
Less refined carbs	◯	◯	◯	◯	◯	◯	◯
Keep notes of triggers	◯	◯	◯	◯	◯	◯	◯
Take Vitamin B12	◯	◯	◯	◯	◯	◯	◯
Take Vitamin D	◯	◯	◯	◯	◯	◯	◯

MY PRIORITIES FOR THIS WEEK

GRATITUDE LOG

MAIN GOALS

DAILY ACTIVITIES

	M	T	W	T	F	S	S
Meditate	○	○	○	○	○	○	○
Exercise	○	○	○	○	○	○	○
Gratitude log	○	○	○	○	○	○	○
Sleep 7+ hours	○	○	○	○	○	○	○
Connect with others	○	○	○	○	○	○	○
Avoid alcohol	○	○	○	○	○	○	○
Less meat	○	○	○	○	○	○	○
Less dairy	○	○	○	○	○	○	○
Less refined carbs	○	○	○	○	○	○	○
Keep notes of triggers	○	○	○	○	○	○	○
Take Vitamin B12	○	○	○	○	○	○	○
Take Vitamin D	○	○	○	○	○	○	○

MY PRIORITIES FOR THIS WEEK

GRATITUDE LOG

MAIN GOALS

DAILY ACTIVITIES

	M	T	W	T	F	S	S
Meditate	○	○	○	○	○	○	○
Exercise	○	○	○	○	○	○	○
Gratitude log	○	○	○	○	○	○	○
Sleep 7+ hours	○	○	○	○	○	○	○
Connect with others	○	○	○	○	○	○	○
Avoid alcohol	○	○	○	○	○	○	○
Less meat	○	○	○	○	○	○	○
Less dairy	○	○	○	○	○	○	○
Less refined carbs	○	○	○	○	○	○	○
Keep notes of triggers	○	○	○	○	○	○	○
Take Vitamin B12	○	○	○	○	○	○	○
Take Vitamin D	○	○	○	○	○	○	○

MY PRIORITIES FOR THIS WEEK

GRATITUDE LOG

MAIN GOALS

DAILY ACTIVITIES

	M	T	W	T	F	S	S
Meditate	○	○	○	○	○	○	○
Exercise	○	○	○	○	○	○	○
Gratitude log	○	○	○	○	○	○	○
Sleep 7+ hours	○	○	○	○	○	○	○
Connect with others	○	○	○	○	○	○	○
Avoid alcohol	○	○	○	○	○	○	○
Less meat	○	○	○	○	○	○	○
Less dairy	○	○	○	○	○	○	○
Less refined carbs	○	○	○	○	○	○	○
Keep notes of triggers	○	○	○	○	○	○	○
Take Vitamin B12	○	○	○	○	○	○	○
Take Vitamin D	○	○	○	○	○	○	○

MY PRIORITIES FOR THIS WEEK

GRATITUDE LOG

MAIN GOALS

DAILY ACTIVITIES

	M	T	W	T	F	S	S
Meditate	○	○	○	○	○	○	○
Exercise	○	○	○	○	○	○	○
Gratitude log	○	○	○	○	○	○	○
Sleep 7+ hours	○	○	○	○	○	○	○
Connect with others	○	○	○	○	○	○	○
Avoid alcohol	○	○	○	○	○	○	○
Less meat	○	○	○	○	○	○	○
Less dairy	○	○	○	○	○	○	○
Less refined carbs	○	○	○	○	○	○	○
Keep notes of triggers	○	○	○	○	○	○	○
Take Vitamin B12	○	○	○	○	○	○	○
Take Vitamin D	○	○	○	○	○	○	○

MY PRIORITIES FOR THIS WEEK

GRATITUDE LOG

MAIN GOALS

DAILY ACTIVITIES

	M	T	W	T	F	S	S
Meditate	○	○	○	○	○	○	○
Exercise	○	○	○	○	○	○	○
Gratitude log	○	○	○	○	○	○	○
Sleep 7+ hours	○	○	○	○	○	○	○
Connect with others	○	○	○	○	○	○	○
Avoid alcohol	○	○	○	○	○	○	○
Less meat	○	○	○	○	○	○	○
Less dairy	○	○	○	○	○	○	○
Less refined carbs	○	○	○	○	○	○	○
Keep notes of triggers	○	○	○	○	○	○	○
Take Vitamin B12	○	○	○	○	○	○	○
Take Vitamin D	○	○	○	○	○	○	○

MY PRIORITIES FOR THIS WEEK

GRATITUDE LOG

MAIN GOALS

DAILY ACTIVITIES

	M	T	W	T	F	S	S
Meditate	◯	◯	◯	◯	◯	◯	◯
Exercise	◯	◯	◯	◯	◯	◯	◯
Gratitude log	◯	◯	◯	◯	◯	◯	◯
Sleep 7+ hours	◯	◯	◯	◯	◯	◯	◯
Connect with others	◯	◯	◯	◯	◯	◯	◯
Avoid alcohol	◯	◯	◯	◯	◯	◯	◯
Less meat	◯	◯	◯	◯	◯	◯	◯
Less dairy	◯	◯	◯	◯	◯	◯	◯
Less refined carbs	◯	◯	◯	◯	◯	◯	◯
Keep notes of triggers	◯	◯	◯	◯	◯	◯	◯
Take Vitamin B12	◯	◯	◯	◯	◯	◯	◯
Take Vitamin D	◯	◯	◯	◯	◯	◯	◯

MY PRIORITIES FOR THIS WEEK

GRATITUDE LOG

MAIN GOALS

DAILY ACTIVITIES

	M	T	W	T	F	S	S
Meditate	○	○	○	○	○	○	○
Exercise	○	○	○	○	○	○	○
Gratitude log	○	○	○	○	○	○	○
Sleep 7+ hours	○	○	○	○	○	○	○
Connect with others	○	○	○	○	○	○	○
Avoid alcohol	○	○	○	○	○	○	○
Less meat	○	○	○	○	○	○	○
Less dairy	○	○	○	○	○	○	○
Less refined carbs	○	○	○	○	○	○	○
Keep notes of triggers	○	○	○	○	○	○	○
Take Vitamin B12	○	○	○	○	○	○	○
Take Vitamin D	○	○	○	○	○	○	○

EAT CLEAN & EXERCISE
STAY
HEALTHY

MY PRIORITIES FOR THIS WEEK

GRATITUDE LOG

MAIN GOALS

DAILY ACTIVITIES

	M	T	W	T	F	S	S
Meditate	○	○	○	○	○	○	○
Exercise	○	○	○	○	○	○	○
Gratitude log	○	○	○	○	○	○	○
Sleep 7+ hours	○	○	○	○	○	○	○
Connect with others	○	○	○	○	○	○	○
Avoid alcohol	○	○	○	○	○	○	○
Less meat	○	○	○	○	○	○	○
Less dairy	○	○	○	○	○	○	○
Less refined carbs	○	○	○	○	○	○	○
Keep notes of triggers	○	○	○	○	○	○	○
Take Vitamin B12	○	○	○	○	○	○	○
Take Vitamin D	○	○	○	○	○	○	○

MY PRIORITIES FOR THIS WEEK

GRATITUDE LOG

MAIN GOALS

DAILY ACTIVITIES

	M	T	W	T	F	S	S
Meditate	○	○	○	○	○	○	○
Exercise	○	○	○	○	○	○	○
Gratitude log	○	○	○	○	○	○	○
Sleep 7+ hours	○	○	○	○	○	○	○
Connect with others	○	○	○	○	○	○	○
Avoid alcohol	○	○	○	○	○	○	○
Less meat	○	○	○	○	○	○	○
Less dairy	○	○	○	○	○	○	○
Less refined carbs	○	○	○	○	○	○	○
Keep notes of triggers	○	○	○	○	○	○	○
Take Vitamin B12	○	○	○	○	○	○	○
Take Vitamin D	○	○	○	○	○	○	○

MY PRIORITIES FOR THIS WEEK

GRATITUDE LOG

MAIN GOALS

DAILY ACTIVITIES

	M	T	W	T	F	S	S
Meditate	○	○	○	○	○	○	○
Exercise	○	○	○	○	○	○	○
Gratitude log	○	○	○	○	○	○	○
Sleep 7+ hours	○	○	○	○	○	○	○
Connect with others	○	○	○	○	○	○	○
Avoid alcohol	○	○	○	○	○	○	○
Less meat	○	○	○	○	○	○	○
Less dairy	○	○	○	○	○	○	○
Less refined carbs	○	○	○	○	○	○	○
Keep notes of triggers	○	○	○	○	○	○	○
Take Vitamin B12	○	○	○	○	○	○	○
Take Vitamin D	○	○	○	○	○	○	○

WEEK OF:

MY PRIORITIES FOR THIS WEEK

GRATITUDE LOG

MAIN GOALS

DAILY ACTIVITIES

M T W T F S S

Meditate
Exercise
Gratitude log
Sleep 7+ hours
Connect with others
Avoid alcohol
Less meat
Less dairy
Less refined carbs
Keep notes of
triggers
Take Vitamin B12
Take Vitamin D

MY PRIORITIES FOR THIS WEEK

GRATITUDE LOG

MAIN GOALS

DAILY ACTIVITIES

	M	T	W	T	F	S	S
Meditate	○	○	○	○	○	○	○
Exercise	○	○	○	○	○	○	○
Gratitude log	○	○	○	○	○	○	○
Sleep 7+ hours	○	○	○	○	○	○	○
Connect with others	○	○	○	○	○	○	○
Avoid alcohol	○	○	○	○	○	○	○
Less meat	○	○	○	○	○	○	○
Less dairy	○	○	○	○	○	○	○
Less refined carbs	○	○	○	○	○	○	○
Keep notes of triggers	○	○	○	○	○	○	○
Take Vitamin B12	○	○	○	○	○	○	○
Take Vitamin D	○	○	○	○	○	○	○

WEEK OF:

MY PRIORITIES FOR THIS WEEK

GRATITUDE LOG

MAIN GOALS

DAILY ACTIVITIES

M T W T F S S

Meditate
Exercise
Gratitude log
Sleep 7+ hours
Connect with others
Avoid alcohol
Less meat
Less dairy
Less refined carbs
Keep notes of triggers
Take Vitamin B12
Take Vitamin D

WEEK OF:

MY PRIORITIES FOR THIS WEEK

GRATITUDE LOG

MAIN GOALS

DAILY ACTIVITIES

M T W T F S S

Meditate
Exercise
Gratitude log
Sleep 7+ hours
Connect with others
Avoid alcohol
Less meat
Less dairy
Less refined carbs
Keep notes of triggers
Take Vitamin B12
Take Vitamin D

WEEK OF:

MY PRIORITIES FOR THIS WEEK

GRATITUDE LOG

MAIN GOALS

DAILY ACTIVITIES

M T W T F S S

Meditate
Exercise
Gratitude log
Sleep 7+ hours
Connect with others
Avoid alcohol
Less meat
Less dairy
Less refined carbs
Keep notes of
triggers
Take Vitamin B12
Take Vitamin D

MY PRIORITIES FOR THIS WEEK

GRATITUDE LOG

MAIN GOALS

DAILY ACTIVITIES

	M	T	W	T	F	S	S
Meditate	○	○	○	○	○	○	○
Exercise	○	○	○	○	○	○	○
Gratitude log	○	○	○	○	○	○	○
Sleep 7+ hours	○	○	○	○	○	○	○
Connect with others	○	○	○	○	○	○	○
Avoid alcohol	○	○	○	○	○	○	○
Less meat	○	○	○	○	○	○	○
Less dairy	○	○	○	○	○	○	○
Less refined carbs	○	○	○	○	○	○	○
Keep notes of triggers	○	○	○	○	○	○	○
Take Vitamin B12	○	○	○	○	○	○	○
Take Vitamin D	○	○	○	○	○	○	○

MY PRIORITIES FOR THIS WEEK

GRATITUDE LOG

MAIN GOALS

DAILY ACTIVITIES

	M	T	W	T	F	S	S
Meditate	○	○	○	○	○	○	○
Exercise	○	○	○	○	○	○	○
Gratitude log	○	○	○	○	○	○	○
Sleep 7+ hours	○	○	○	○	○	○	○
Connect with others	○	○	○	○	○	○	○
Avoid alcohol	○	○	○	○	○	○	○
Less meat	○	○	○	○	○	○	○
Less dairy	○	○	○	○	○	○	○
Less refined carbs	○	○	○	○	○	○	○
Keep notes of triggers	○	○	○	○	○	○	○
Take Vitamin B12	○	○	○	○	○	○	○
Take Vitamin D	○	○	○	○	○	○	○

MY PRIORITIES FOR THIS WEEK

GRATITUDE LOG

MAIN GOALS

DAILY ACTIVITIES

	M	T	W	T	F	S	S
Meditate	○	○	○	○	○	○	○
Exercise	○	○	○	○	○	○	○
Gratitude log	○	○	○	○	○	○	○
Sleep 7+ hours	○	○	○	○	○	○	○
Connect with others	○	○	○	○	○	○	○
Avoid alcohol	○	○	○	○	○	○	○
Less meat	○	○	○	○	○	○	○
Less dairy	○	○	○	○	○	○	○
Less refined carbs	○	○	○	○	○	○	○
Keep notes of triggers	○	○	○	○	○	○	○
Take Vitamin B12	○	○	○	○	○	○	○
Take Vitamin D	○	○	○	○	○	○	○

MY PRIORITIES FOR THIS WEEK

GRATITUDE LOG

MAIN GOALS

DAILY ACTIVITIES

	M	T	W	T	F	S	S
Meditate	◯	◯	◯	◯	◯	◯	◯
Exercise	◯	◯	◯	◯	◯	◯	◯
Gratitude log	◯	◯	◯	◯	◯	◯	◯
Sleep 7+ hours	◯	◯	◯	◯	◯	◯	◯
Connect with others	◯	◯	◯	◯	◯	◯	◯
Avoid alcohol	◯	◯	◯	◯	◯	◯	◯
Less meat	◯	◯	◯	◯	◯	◯	◯
Less dairy	◯	◯	◯	◯	◯	◯	◯
Less refined carbs	◯	◯	◯	◯	◯	◯	◯
Keep notes of triggers	◯	◯	◯	◯	◯	◯	◯
Take Vitamin B12	◯	◯	◯	◯	◯	◯	◯
Take Vitamin D	◯	◯	◯	◯	◯	◯	◯

WEEK OF:

MY PRIORITIES FOR THIS WEEK

GRATITUDE LOG

MAIN GOALS

DAILY ACTIVITIES

M T W T F S S

Meditate
Exercise
Gratitude log
Sleep 7+ hours
Connect with others
Avoid alcohol
Less meat
Less dairy
Less refined carbs
Keep notes of triggers
Take Vitamin B12
Take Vitamin D

MY PRIORITIES FOR THIS WEEK

GRATITUDE LOG

MAIN GOALS

DAILY ACTIVITIES

	M	T	W	T	F	S	S
Meditate	○	○	○	○	○	○	○
Exercise	○	○	○	○	○	○	○
Gratitude log	○	○	○	○	○	○	○
Sleep 7+ hours	○	○	○	○	○	○	○
Connect with others	○	○	○	○	○	○	○
Avoid alcohol	○	○	○	○	○	○	○
Less meat	○	○	○	○	○	○	○
Less dairy	○	○	○	○	○	○	○
Less refined carbs	○	○	○	○	○	○	○
Keep notes of triggers	○	○	○	○	○	○	○
Take Vitamin B12	○	○	○	○	○	○	○
Take Vitamin D	○	○	○	○	○	○	○

MY PRIORITIES FOR THIS WEEK

GRATITUDE LOG

MAIN GOALS

DAILY ACTIVITIES

	M	T	W	T	F	S	S
Meditate	○	○	○	○	○	○	○
Exercise	○	○	○	○	○	○	○
Gratitude log	○	○	○	○	○	○	○
Sleep 7+ hours	○	○	○	○	○	○	○
Connect with others	○	○	○	○	○	○	○
Avoid alcohol	○	○	○	○	○	○	○
Less meat	○	○	○	○	○	○	○
Less dairy	○	○	○	○	○	○	○
Less refined carbs	○	○	○	○	○	○	○
Keep notes of triggers	○	○	○	○	○	○	○
Take Vitamin B12	○	○	○	○	○	○	○
Take Vitamin D	○	○	○	○	○	○	○

MY PRIORITIES FOR THIS WEEK

GRATITUDE LOG

MAIN GOALS

DAILY ACTIVITIES

	M	T	W	T	F	S	S
Meditate	◯	◯	◯	◯	◯	◯	◯
Exercise	◯	◯	◯	◯	◯	◯	◯
Gratitude log	◯	◯	◯	◯	◯	◯	◯
Sleep 7+ hours	◯	◯	◯	◯	◯	◯	◯
Connect with others	◯	◯	◯	◯	◯	◯	◯
Avoid alcohol	◯	◯	◯	◯	◯	◯	◯
Less meat	◯	◯	◯	◯	◯	◯	◯
Less dairy	◯	◯	◯	◯	◯	◯	◯
Less refined carbs	◯	◯	◯	◯	◯	◯	◯
Keep notes of triggers	◯	◯	◯	◯	◯	◯	◯
Take Vitamin B12	◯	◯	◯	◯	◯	◯	◯
Take Vitamin D	◯	◯	◯	◯	◯	◯	◯

MY PRIORITIES FOR THIS WEEK

GRATITUDE LOG

MAIN GOALS

DAILY ACTIVITIES

	M	T	W	T	F	S	S
Meditate	○	○	○	○	○	○	○
Exercise	○	○	○	○	○	○	○
Gratitude log	○	○	○	○	○	○	○
Sleep 7+ hours	○	○	○	○	○	○	○
Connect with others	○	○	○	○	○	○	○
Avoid alcohol	○	○	○	○	○	○	○
Less meat	○	○	○	○	○	○	○
Less dairy	○	○	○	○	○	○	○
Less refined carbs	○	○	○	○	○	○	○
Keep notes of triggers	○	○	○	○	○	○	○
Take Vitamin B12	○	○	○	○	○	○	○
Take Vitamin D	○	○	○	○	○	○	○

WEEK OF:

MY PRIORITIES FOR THIS WEEK

GRATITUDE LOG

MAIN GOALS

DAILY ACTIVITIES

M T W T F S S

Meditate
Exercise
Gratitude log
Sleep 7+ hours
Connect with others
Avoid alcohol
Less meat
Less dairy
Less refined carbs
Keep notes of triggers
Take Vitamin B12
Take Vitamin D

MY PRIORITIES FOR THIS WEEK

GRATITUDE LOG

MAIN GOALS

DAILY ACTIVITIES

	M	T	W	T	F	S	S
Meditate	○	○	○	○	○	○	○
Exercise	○	○	○	○	○	○	○
Gratitude log	○	○	○	○	○	○	○
Sleep 7+ hours	○	○	○	○	○	○	○
Connect with others	○	○	○	○	○	○	○
Avoid alcohol	○	○	○	○	○	○	○
Less meat	○	○	○	○	○	○	○
Less dairy	○	○	○	○	○	○	○
Less refined carbs	○	○	○	○	○	○	○
Keep notes of triggers	○	○	○	○	○	○	○
Take Vitamin B12	○	○	○	○	○	○	○
Take Vitamin D	○	○	○	○	○	○	○

MY PRIORITIES FOR THIS WEEK

GRATITUDE LOG

MAIN GOALS

DAILY ACTIVITIES

	M	T	W	T	F	S	S
Meditate	○	○	○	○	○	○	○
Exercise	○	○	○	○	○	○	○
Gratitude log	○	○	○	○	○	○	○
Sleep 7+ hours	○	○	○	○	○	○	○
Connect with others	○	○	○	○	○	○	○
Avoid alcohol	○	○	○	○	○	○	○
Less meat	○	○	○	○	○	○	○
Less dairy	○	○	○	○	○	○	○
Less refined carbs	○	○	○	○	○	○	○
Keep notes of triggers	○	○	○	○	○	○	○
Take Vitamin B12	○	○	○	○	○	○	○
Take Vitamin D	○	○	○	○	○	○	○

MY PRIORITIES FOR THIS WEEK

GRATITUDE LOG

MAIN GOALS

DAILY ACTIVITIES

	M	T	W	T	F	S	S
Meditate	○	○	○	○	○	○	○
Exercise	○	○	○	○	○	○	○
Gratitude log	○	○	○	○	○	○	○
Sleep 7+ hours	○	○	○	○	○	○	○
Connect with others	○	○	○	○	○	○	○
Avoid alcohol	○	○	○	○	○	○	○
Less meat	○	○	○	○	○	○	○
Less dairy	○	○	○	○	○	○	○
Less refined carbs	○	○	○	○	○	○	○
Keep notes of triggers	○	○	○	○	○	○	○
Take Vitamin B12	○	○	○	○	○	○	○
Take Vitamin D	○	○	○	○	○	○	○

MY PRIORITIES FOR THIS WEEK

GRATITUDE LOG

MAIN GOALS

DAILY ACTIVITIES

	M	T	W	T	F	S	S
Meditate	○	○	○	○	○	○	○
Exercise	○	○	○	○	○	○	○
Gratitude log	○	○	○	○	○	○	○
Sleep 7+ hours	○	○	○	○	○	○	○
Connect with others	○	○	○	○	○	○	○
Avoid alcohol	○	○	○	○	○	○	○
Less meat	○	○	○	○	○	○	○
Less dairy	○	○	○	○	○	○	○
Less refined carbs	○	○	○	○	○	○	○
Keep notes of triggers	○	○	○	○	○	○	○
Take Vitamin B12	○	○	○	○	○	○	○
Take Vitamin D	○	○	○	○	○	○	○

MY PRIORITIES FOR THIS WEEK

GRATITUDE LOG

MAIN GOALS

DAILY ACTIVITIES

	M	T	W	T	F	S	S
Meditate	○	○	○	○	○	○	○
Exercise	○	○	○	○	○	○	○
Gratitude log	○	○	○	○	○	○	○
Sleep 7+ hours	○	○	○	○	○	○	○
Connect with others	○	○	○	○	○	○	○
Avoid alcohol	○	○	○	○	○	○	○
Less meat	○	○	○	○	○	○	○
Less dairy	○	○	○	○	○	○	○
Less refined carbs	○	○	○	○	○	○	○
Keep notes of triggers	○	○	○	○	○	○	○
Take Vitamin B12	○	○	○	○	○	○	○
Take Vitamin D	○	○	○	○	○	○	○

MY PRIORITIES FOR THIS WEEK

GRATITUDE LOG

MAIN GOALS

DAILY ACTIVITIES

	M	T	W	T	F	S	S
Meditate	○	○	○	○	○	○	○
Exercise	○	○	○	○	○	○	○
Gratitude log	○	○	○	○	○	○	○
Sleep 7+ hours	○	○	○	○	○	○	○
Connect with others	○	○	○	○	○	○	○
Avoid alcohol	○	○	○	○	○	○	○
Less meat	○	○	○	○	○	○	○
Less dairy	○	○	○	○	○	○	○
Less refined carbs	○	○	○	○	○	○	○
Keep notes of triggers	○	○	○	○	○	○	○
Take Vitamin B12	○	○	○	○	○	○	○
Take Vitamin D	○	○	○	○	○	○	○

MY PRIORITIES FOR THIS WEEK

GRATITUDE LOG

MAIN GOALS

DAILY ACTIVITIES

	M	T	W	T	F	S	S
Meditate	○	○	○	○	○	○	○
Exercise	○	○	○	○	○	○	○
Gratitude log	○	○	○	○	○	○	○
Sleep 7+ hours	○	○	○	○	○	○	○
Connect with others	○	○	○	○	○	○	○
Avoid alcohol	○	○	○	○	○	○	○
Less meat	○	○	○	○	○	○	○
Less dairy	○	○	○	○	○	○	○
Less refined carbs	○	○	○	○	○	○	○
Keep notes of triggers	○	○	○	○	○	○	○
Take Vitamin B12	○	○	○	○	○	○	○
Take Vitamin D	○	○	○	○	○	○	○

MY PRIORITIES FOR THIS WEEK

GRATITUDE LOG

MAIN GOALS

DAILY ACTIVITIES

	M	T	W	T	F	S	S
Meditate	○	○	○	○	○	○	○
Exercise	○	○	○	○	○	○	○
Gratitude log	○	○	○	○	○	○	○
Sleep 7+ hours	○	○	○	○	○	○	○
Connect with others	○	○	○	○	○	○	○
Avoid alcohol	○	○	○	○	○	○	○
Less meat	○	○	○	○	○	○	○
Less dairy	○	○	○	○	○	○	○
Less refined carbs	○	○	○	○	○	○	○
Keep notes of triggers	○	○	○	○	○	○	○
Take Vitamin B12	○	○	○	○	○	○	○
Take Vitamin D	○	○	○	○	○	○	○

MY PRIORITIES FOR THIS WEEK

GRATITUDE LOG

MAIN GOALS

DAILY ACTIVITIES

	M	T	W	T	F	S	S
Meditate	○	○	○	○	○	○	○
Exercise	○	○	○	○	○	○	○
Gratitude log	○	○	○	○	○	○	○
Sleep 7+ hours	○	○	○	○	○	○	○
Connect with others	○	○	○	○	○	○	○
Avoid alcohol	○	○	○	○	○	○	○
Less meat	○	○	○	○	○	○	○
Less dairy	○	○	○	○	○	○	○
Less refined carbs	○	○	○	○	○	○	○
Keep notes of triggers	○	○	○	○	○	○	○
Take Vitamin B12	○	○	○	○	○	○	○
Take Vitamin D	○	○	○	○	○	○	○

MY PRIORITIES FOR THIS WEEK

GRATITUDE LOG

MAIN GOALS

DAILY ACTIVITIES

	M	T	W	T	F	S	S
Meditate	○	○	○	○	○	○	○
Exercise	○	○	○	○	○	○	○
Gratitude log	○	○	○	○	○	○	○
Sleep 7+ hours	○	○	○	○	○	○	○
Connect with others	○	○	○	○	○	○	○
Avoid alcohol	○	○	○	○	○	○	○
Less meat	○	○	○	○	○	○	○
Less dairy	○	○	○	○	○	○	○
Less refined carbs	○	○	○	○	○	○	○
Keep notes of triggers	○	○	○	○	○	○	○
Take Vitamin B12	○	○	○	○	○	○	○
Take Vitamin D	○	○	○	○	○	○	○

MY PRIORITIES FOR THIS WEEK

GRATITUDE LOG

MAIN GOALS

DAILY ACTIVITIES

	M	T	W	T	F	S	S
Meditate	○	○	○	○	○	○	○
Exercise	○	○	○	○	○	○	○
Gratitude log	○	○	○	○	○	○	○
Sleep 7+ hours	○	○	○	○	○	○	○
Connect with others	○	○	○	○	○	○	○
Avoid alcohol	○	○	○	○	○	○	○
Less meat	○	○	○	○	○	○	○
Less dairy	○	○	○	○	○	○	○
Less refined carbs	○	○	○	○	○	○	○
Keep notes of triggers	○	○	○	○	○	○	○
Take Vitamin B12	○	○	○	○	○	○	○
Take Vitamin D	○	○	○	○	○	○	○

MY PRIORITIES FOR THIS WEEK

GRATITUDE LOG

MAIN GOALS

DAILY ACTIVITIES

	M	T	W	T	F	S	S
Meditate	◯	◯	◯	◯	◯	◯	◯
Exercise	◯	◯	◯	◯	◯	◯	◯
Gratitude log	◯	◯	◯	◯	◯	◯	◯
Sleep 7+ hours	◯	◯	◯	◯	◯	◯	◯
Connect with others	◯	◯	◯	◯	◯	◯	◯
Avoid alcohol	◯	◯	◯	◯	◯	◯	◯
Less meat	◯	◯	◯	◯	◯	◯	◯
Less dairy	◯	◯	◯	◯	◯	◯	◯
Less refined carbs	◯	◯	◯	◯	◯	◯	◯
Keep notes of triggers	◯	◯	◯	◯	◯	◯	◯
Take Vitamin B12	◯	◯	◯	◯	◯	◯	◯
Take Vitamin D	◯	◯	◯	◯	◯	◯	◯

WEEK OF:

MY PRIORITIES FOR THIS WEEK

GRATITUDE LOG

MAIN GOALS

DAILY ACTIVITIES

M T W T F S S

Meditate
Exercise
Gratitude log
Sleep 7+ hours
Connect with others
Avoid alcohol
Less meat
Less dairy
Less refined carbs
Keep notes of
triggers
Take Vitamin B12
Take Vitamin D

MY PRIORITIES FOR THIS WEEK

GRATITUDE LOG

MAIN GOALS

DAILY ACTIVITIES

	M	T	W	T	F	S	S
Meditate	○	○	○	○	○	○	○
Exercise	○	○	○	○	○	○	○
Gratitude log	○	○	○	○	○	○	○
Sleep 7+ hours	○	○	○	○	○	○	○
Connect with others	○	○	○	○	○	○	○
Avoid alcohol	○	○	○	○	○	○	○
Less meat	○	○	○	○	○	○	○
Less dairy	○	○	○	○	○	○	○
Less refined carbs	○	○	○	○	○	○	○
Keep notes of triggers	○	○	○	○	○	○	○
Take Vitamin B12	○	○	○	○	○	○	○
Take Vitamin D	○	○	○	○	○	○	○

MY PRIORITIES FOR THIS WEEK

GRATITUDE LOG

MAIN GOALS

DAILY ACTIVITIES

	M	T	W	T	F	S	S
Meditate	○	○	○	○	○	○	○
Exercise	○	○	○	○	○	○	○
Gratitude log	○	○	○	○	○	○	○
Sleep 7+ hours	○	○	○	○	○	○	○
Connect with others	○	○	○	○	○	○	○
Avoid alcohol	○	○	○	○	○	○	○
Less meat	○	○	○	○	○	○	○
Less dairy	○	○	○	○	○	○	○
Less refined carbs	○	○	○	○	○	○	○
Keep notes of triggers	○	○	○	○	○	○	○
Take Vitamin B12	○	○	○	○	○	○	○
Take Vitamin D	○	○	○	○	○	○	○

MY PRIORITIES FOR THIS WEEK

GRATITUDE LOG

MAIN GOALS

DAILY ACTIVITIES

	M	T	W	T	F	S	S
Meditate	○	○	○	○	○	○	○
Exercise	○	○	○	○	○	○	○
Gratitude log	○	○	○	○	○	○	○
Sleep 7+ hours	○	○	○	○	○	○	○
Connect with others	○	○	○	○	○	○	○
Avoid alcohol	○	○	○	○	○	○	○
Less meat	○	○	○	○	○	○	○
Less dairy	○	○	○	○	○	○	○
Less refined carbs	○	○	○	○	○	○	○
Keep notes of triggers	○	○	○	○	○	○	○
Take Vitamin B12	○	○	○	○	○	○	○
Take Vitamin D	○	○	○	○	○	○	○

MY PRIORITIES FOR THIS WEEK

GRATITUDE LOG

MAIN GOALS

DAILY ACTIVITIES

	M	T	W	T	F	S	S
Meditate	○	○	○	○	○	○	○
Exercise	○	○	○	○	○	○	○
Gratitude log	○	○	○	○	○	○	○
Sleep 7+ hours	○	○	○	○	○	○	○
Connect with others	○	○	○	○	○	○	○
Avoid alcohol	○	○	○	○	○	○	○
Less meat	○	○	○	○	○	○	○
Less dairy	○	○	○	○	○	○	○
Less refined carbs	○	○	○	○	○	○	○
Keep notes of triggers	○	○	○	○	○	○	○
Take Vitamin B12	○	○	○	○	○	○	○
Take Vitamin D	○	○	○	○	○	○	○

MY PRIORITIES FOR THIS WEEK

GRATITUDE LOG

MAIN GOALS

DAILY ACTIVITIES

	M	T	W	T	F	S	S
Meditate	○	○	○	○	○	○	○
Exercise	○	○	○	○	○	○	○
Gratitude log	○	○	○	○	○	○	○
Sleep 7+ hours	○	○	○	○	○	○	○
Connect with others	○	○	○	○	○	○	○
Avoid alcohol	○	○	○	○	○	○	○
Less meat	○	○	○	○	○	○	○
Less dairy	○	○	○	○	○	○	○
Less refined carbs	○	○	○	○	○	○	○
Keep notes of triggers	○	○	○	○	○	○	○
Take Vitamin B12	○	○	○	○	○	○	○
Take Vitamin D	○	○	○	○	○	○	○

WEEK OF:

MY PRIORITIES FOR THIS WEEK

GRATITUDE LOG

MAIN GOALS

DAILY ACTIVITIES

M T W T F S S

Meditate
Exercise
Gratitude log
Sleep 7+ hours
Connect with others
Avoid alcohol
Less meat
Less dairy
Less refined carbs
Keep notes of
triggers
Take Vitamin B12
Take Vitamin D

MY PRIORITIES FOR THIS WEEK

GRATITUDE LOG

MAIN GOALS

DAILY ACTIVITIES

	M	T	W	T	F	S	S
Meditate	○	○	○	○	○	○	○
Exercise	○	○	○	○	○	○	○
Gratitude log	○	○	○	○	○	○	○
Sleep 7+ hours	○	○	○	○	○	○	○
Connect with others	○	○	○	○	○	○	○
Avoid alcohol	○	○	○	○	○	○	○
Less meat	○	○	○	○	○	○	○
Less dairy	○	○	○	○	○	○	○
Less refined carbs	○	○	○	○	○	○	○
Keep notes of triggers	○	○	○	○	○	○	○
Take Vitamin B12	○	○	○	○	○	○	○
Take Vitamin D	○	○	○	○	○	○	○

MY PRIORITIES FOR THIS WEEK

GRATITUDE LOG

MAIN GOALS

DAILY ACTIVITIES

	M	T	W	T	F	S	S
Meditate	○	○	○	○	○	○	○
Exercise	○	○	○	○	○	○	○
Gratitude log	○	○	○	○	○	○	○
Sleep 7+ hours	○	○	○	○	○	○	○
Connect with others	○	○	○	○	○	○	○
Avoid alcohol	○	○	○	○	○	○	○
Less meat	○	○	○	○	○	○	○
Less dairy	○	○	○	○	○	○	○
Less refined carbs	○	○	○	○	○	○	○
Keep notes of triggers	○	○	○	○	○	○	○
Take Vitamin B12	○	○	○	○	○	○	○
Take Vitamin D	○	○	○	○	○	○	○

MY PRIORITIES FOR THIS WEEK

GRATITUDE LOG

MAIN GOALS

DAILY ACTIVITIES

	M	T	W	T	F	S	S
Meditate	○	○	○	○	○	○	○
Exercise	○	○	○	○	○	○	○
Gratitude log	○	○	○	○	○	○	○
Sleep 7+ hours	○	○	○	○	○	○	○
Connect with others	○	○	○	○	○	○	○
Avoid alcohol	○	○	○	○	○	○	○
Less meat	○	○	○	○	○	○	○
Less dairy	○	○	○	○	○	○	○
Less refined carbs	○	○	○	○	○	○	○
Keep notes of triggers	○	○	○	○	○	○	○
Take Vitamin B12	○	○	○	○	○	○	○
Take Vitamin D	○	○	○	○	○	○	○

MY PRIORITIES FOR THIS WEEK

GRATITUDE LOG

MAIN GOALS

DAILY ACTIVITIES

	M	T	W	T	F	S	S
Meditate	○	○	○	○	○	○	○
Exercise	○	○	○	○	○	○	○
Gratitude log	○	○	○	○	○	○	○
Sleep 7+ hours	○	○	○	○	○	○	○
Connect with others	○	○	○	○	○	○	○
Avoid alcohol	○	○	○	○	○	○	○
Less meat	○	○	○	○	○	○	○
Less dairy	○	○	○	○	○	○	○
Less refined carbs	○	○	○	○	○	○	○
Keep notes of triggers	○	○	○	○	○	○	○
Take Vitamin B12	○	○	○	○	○	○	○
Take Vitamin D	○	○	○	○	○	○	○

MY PRIORITIES FOR THIS WEEK

GRATITUDE LOG

MAIN GOALS

DAILY ACTIVITIES

	M	T	W	T	F	S	S
Meditate	○	○	○	○	○	○	○
Exercise	○	○	○	○	○	○	○
Gratitude log	○	○	○	○	○	○	○
Sleep 7+ hours	○	○	○	○	○	○	○
Connect with others	○	○	○	○	○	○	○
Avoid alcohol	○	○	○	○	○	○	○
Less meat	○	○	○	○	○	○	○
Less dairy	○	○	○	○	○	○	○
Less refined carbs	○	○	○	○	○	○	○
Keep notes of triggers	○	○	○	○	○	○	○
Take Vitamin B12	○	○	○	○	○	○	○
Take Vitamin D	○	○	○	○	○	○	○

MY PRIORITIES FOR THIS WEEK

GRATITUDE LOG

MAIN GOALS

DAILY ACTIVITIES

	M	T	W	T	F	S	S
Meditate	○	○	○	○	○	○	○
Exercise	○	○	○	○	○	○	○
Gratitude log	○	○	○	○	○	○	○
Sleep 7+ hours	○	○	○	○	○	○	○
Connect with others	○	○	○	○	○	○	○
Avoid alcohol	○	○	○	○	○	○	○
Less meat	○	○	○	○	○	○	○
Less dairy	○	○	○	○	○	○	○
Less refined carbs	○	○	○	○	○	○	○
Keep notes of triggers	○	○	○	○	○	○	○
Take Vitamin B12	○	○	○	○	○	○	○
Take Vitamin D	○	○	○	○	○	○	○

MY PRIORITIES FOR THIS WEEK

GRATITUDE LOG

MAIN GOALS

DAILY ACTIVITIES

	M	T	W	T	F	S	S
Meditate	○	○	○	○	○	○	○
Exercise	○	○	○	○	○	○	○
Gratitude log	○	○	○	○	○	○	○
Sleep 7+ hours	○	○	○	○	○	○	○
Connect with others	○	○	○	○	○	○	○
Avoid alcohol	○	○	○	○	○	○	○
Less meat	○	○	○	○	○	○	○
Less dairy	○	○	○	○	○	○	○
Less refined carbs	○	○	○	○	○	○	○
Keep notes of triggers	○	○	○	○	○	○	○
Take Vitamin B12	○	○	○	○	○	○	○
Take Vitamin D	○	○	○	○	○	○	○

MY PRIORITIES FOR THIS WEEK

GRATITUDE LOG

MAIN GOALS

DAILY ACTIVITIES

	M	T	W	T	F	S	S
Meditate	○	○	○	○	○	○	○
Exercise	○	○	○	○	○	○	○
Gratitude log	○	○	○	○	○	○	○
Sleep 7+ hours	○	○	○	○	○	○	○
Connect with others	○	○	○	○	○	○	○
Avoid alcohol	○	○	○	○	○	○	○
Less meat	○	○	○	○	○	○	○
Less dairy	○	○	○	○	○	○	○
Less refined carbs	○	○	○	○	○	○	○
Keep notes of triggers	○	○	○	○	○	○	○
Take Vitamin B12	○	○	○	○	○	○	○
Take Vitamin D	○	○	○	○	○	○	○

MY PRIORITIES FOR THIS WEEK

GRATITUDE LOG

MAIN GOALS

DAILY ACTIVITIES

	M	T	W	T	F	S	S
Meditate	○	○	○	○	○	○	○
Exercise	○	○	○	○	○	○	○
Gratitude log	○	○	○	○	○	○	○
Sleep 7+ hours	○	○	○	○	○	○	○
Connect with others	○	○	○	○	○	○	○
Avoid alcohol	○	○	○	○	○	○	○
Less meat	○	○	○	○	○	○	○
Less dairy	○	○	○	○	○	○	○
Less refined carbs	○	○	○	○	○	○	○
Keep notes of triggers	○	○	○	○	○	○	○
Take Vitamin B12	○	○	○	○	○	○	○
Take Vitamin D	○	○	○	○	○	○	○

MY PRIORITIES FOR THIS WEEK

GRATITUDE LOG

MAIN GOALS

DAILY ACTIVITIES

	M	T	W	T	F	S	S
Meditate	○	○	○	○	○	○	○
Exercise	○	○	○	○	○	○	○
Gratitude log	○	○	○	○	○	○	○
Sleep 7+ hours	○	○	○	○	○	○	○
Connect with others	○	○	○	○	○	○	○
Avoid alcohol	○	○	○	○	○	○	○
Less meat	○	○	○	○	○	○	○
Less dairy	○	○	○	○	○	○	○
Less refined carbs	○	○	○	○	○	○	○
Keep notes of triggers	○	○	○	○	○	○	○
Take Vitamin B12	○	○	○	○	○	○	○
Take Vitamin D	○	○	○	○	○	○	○

MY PRIORITIES FOR THIS WEEK

GRATITUDE LOG

MAIN GOALS

DAILY ACTIVITIES

	M	T	W	T	F	S	S
Meditate	○	○	○	○	○	○	○
Exercise	○	○	○	○	○	○	○
Gratitude log	○	○	○	○	○	○	○
Sleep 7+ hours	○	○	○	○	○	○	○
Connect with others	○	○	○	○	○	○	○
Avoid alcohol	○	○	○	○	○	○	○
Less meat	○	○	○	○	○	○	○
Less dairy	○	○	○	○	○	○	○
Less refined carbs	○	○	○	○	○	○	○
Keep notes of triggers	○	○	○	○	○	○	○
Take Vitamin B12	○	○	○	○	○	○	○
Take Vitamin D	○	○	○	○	○	○	○

MY PRIORITIES FOR THIS WEEK

GRATITUDE LOG

MAIN GOALS

DAILY ACTIVITIES

	M	T	W	T	F	S	S
Meditate	○	○	○	○	○	○	○
Exercise	○	○	○	○	○	○	○
Gratitude log	○	○	○	○	○	○	○
Sleep 7+ hours	○	○	○	○	○	○	○
Connect with others	○	○	○	○	○	○	○
Avoid alcohol	○	○	○	○	○	○	○
Less meat	○	○	○	○	○	○	○
Less dairy	○	○	○	○	○	○	○
Less refined carbs	○	○	○	○	○	○	○
Keep notes of triggers	○	○	○	○	○	○	○
Take Vitamin B12	○	○	○	○	○	○	○
Take Vitamin D	○	○	○	○	○	○	○

MY PRIORITIES FOR THIS WEEK

GRATITUDE LOG

MAIN GOALS

DAILY ACTIVITIES

	M	T	W	T	F	S	S
Meditate	○	○	○	○	○	○	○
Exercise	○	○	○	○	○	○	○
Gratitude log	○	○	○	○	○	○	○
Sleep 7+ hours	○	○	○	○	○	○	○
Connect with others	○	○	○	○	○	○	○
Avoid alcohol	○	○	○	○	○	○	○
Less meat	○	○	○	○	○	○	○
Less dairy	○	○	○	○	○	○	○
Less refined carbs	○	○	○	○	○	○	○
Keep notes of triggers	○	○	○	○	○	○	○
Take Vitamin B12	○	○	○	○	○	○	○
Take Vitamin D	○	○	○	○	○	○	○

MY PRIORITIES FOR THIS WEEK

GRATITUDE LOG

MAIN GOALS

DAILY ACTIVITIES

	M	T	W	T	F	S	S
Meditate	○	○	○	○	○	○	○
Exercise	○	○	○	○	○	○	○
Gratitude log	○	○	○	○	○	○	○
Sleep 7+ hours	○	○	○	○	○	○	○
Connect with others	○	○	○	○	○	○	○
Avoid alcohol	○	○	○	○	○	○	○
Less meat	○	○	○	○	○	○	○
Less dairy	○	○	○	○	○	○	○
Less refined carbs	○	○	○	○	○	○	○
Keep notes of triggers	○	○	○	○	○	○	○
Take Vitamin B12	○	○	○	○	○	○	○
Take Vitamin D	○	○	○	○	○	○	○

MY PRIORITIES FOR THIS WEEK

GRATITUDE LOG

MAIN GOALS

DAILY ACTIVITIES

	M	T	W	T	F	S	S
Meditate	○	○	○	○	○	○	○
Exercise	○	○	○	○	○	○	○
Gratitude log	○	○	○	○	○	○	○
Sleep 7+ hours	○	○	○	○	○	○	○
Connect with others	○	○	○	○	○	○	○
Avoid alcohol	○	○	○	○	○	○	○
Less meat	○	○	○	○	○	○	○
Less dairy	○	○	○	○	○	○	○
Less refined carbs	○	○	○	○	○	○	○
Keep notes of triggers	○	○	○	○	○	○	○
Take Vitamin B12	○	○	○	○	○	○	○
Take Vitamin D	○	○	○	○	○	○	○

EAT CLEAN & EXERCISE
STAY
HEALTHY

MY PRIORITIES FOR THIS WEEK

GRATITUDE LOG

MAIN GOALS

DAILY ACTIVITIES

	M	T	W	T	F	S	S
Meditate	○	○	○	○	○	○	○
Exercise	○	○	○	○	○	○	○
Gratitude log	○	○	○	○	○	○	○
Sleep 7+ hours	○	○	○	○	○	○	○
Connect with others	○	○	○	○	○	○	○
Avoid alcohol	○	○	○	○	○	○	○
Less meat	○	○	○	○	○	○	○
Less dairy	○	○	○	○	○	○	○
Less refined carbs	○	○	○	○	○	○	○
Keep notes of triggers	○	○	○	○	○	○	○
Take Vitamin B12	○	○	○	○	○	○	○
Take Vitamin D	○	○	○	○	○	○	○

WEEK OF:

MY PRIORITIES FOR THIS WEEK

GRATITUDE LOG

MAIN GOALS

DAILY ACTIVITIES

M T W T F S S

Meditate
Exercise
Gratitude log
Sleep 7+ hours
Connect with others
Avoid alcohol
Less meat
Less dairy
Less refined carbs
Keep notes of triggers
Take Vitamin B12
Take Vitamin D

MY PRIORITIES FOR THIS WEEK

GRATITUDE LOG

MAIN GOALS

DAILY ACTIVITIES

	M	T	W	T	F	S	S
Meditate	○	○	○	○	○	○	○
Exercise	○	○	○	○	○	○	○
Gratitude log	○	○	○	○	○	○	○
Sleep 7+ hours	○	○	○	○	○	○	○
Connect with others	○	○	○	○	○	○	○
Avoid alcohol	○	○	○	○	○	○	○
Less meat	○	○	○	○	○	○	○
Less dairy	○	○	○	○	○	○	○
Less refined carbs	○	○	○	○	○	○	○
Keep notes of triggers	○	○	○	○	○	○	○
Take Vitamin B12	○	○	○	○	○	○	○
Take Vitamin D	○	○	○	○	○	○	○

MY PRIORITIES FOR THIS WEEK

GRATITUDE LOG

MAIN GOALS

DAILY ACTIVITIES

	M	T	W	T	F	S	S
Meditate							
Exercise							
Gratitude log							
Sleep 7+ hours							
Connect with others							
Avoid alcohol							
Less meat							
Less dairy							
Less refined carbs							
Keep notes of triggers							
Take Vitamin B12							
Take Vitamin D							

WEEK OF:

MY PRIORITIES FOR THIS WEEK

GRATITUDE LOG

MAIN GOALS

DAILY ACTIVITIES

M T W T F S S

Meditate
Exercise
Gratitude log
Sleep 7+ hours
Connect with others
Avoid alcohol
Less meat
Less dairy
Less refined carbs
Keep notes of triggers
Take Vitamin B12
Take Vitamin D

MY PRIORITIES FOR THIS WEEK

GRATITUDE LOG

MAIN GOALS

DAILY ACTIVITIES

	M	T	W	T	F	S	S
Meditate	○	○	○	○	○	○	○
Exercise	○	○	○	○	○	○	○
Gratitude log	○	○	○	○	○	○	○
Sleep 7+ hours	○	○	○	○	○	○	○
Connect with others	○	○	○	○	○	○	○
Avoid alcohol	○	○	○	○	○	○	○
Less meat	○	○	○	○	○	○	○
Less dairy	○	○	○	○	○	○	○
Less refined carbs	○	○	○	○	○	○	○
Keep notes of triggers	○	○	○	○	○	○	○
Take Vitamin B12	○	○	○	○	○	○	○
Take Vitamin D	○	○	○	○	○	○	○

MY PRIORITIES FOR THIS WEEK

GRATITUDE LOG

MAIN GOALS

DAILY ACTIVITIES

	M	T	W	T	F	S	S
Meditate	○	○	○	○	○	○	○
Exercise	○	○	○	○	○	○	○
Gratitude log	○	○	○	○	○	○	○
Sleep 7+ hours	○	○	○	○	○	○	○
Connect with others	○	○	○	○	○	○	○
Avoid alcohol	○	○	○	○	○	○	○
Less meat	○	○	○	○	○	○	○
Less dairy	○	○	○	○	○	○	○
Less refined carbs	○	○	○	○	○	○	○
Keep notes of triggers	○	○	○	○	○	○	○
Take Vitamin B12	○	○	○	○	○	○	○
Take Vitamin D	○	○	○	○	○	○	○

WEEK OF:

MY PRIORITIES FOR THIS WEEK

GRATITUDE LOG

MAIN GOALS

DAILY ACTIVITIES

M T W T F S S

Meditate
Exercise
Gratitude log
Sleep 7+ hours
Connect with others
Avoid alcohol
Less meat
Less dairy
Less refined carbs
Keep notes of triggers
Take Vitamin B12
Take Vitamin D

WEEK OF:

MY PRIORITIES FOR THIS WEEK

GRATITUDE LOG

MAIN GOALS

DAILY ACTIVITIES

M T W T F S S

Meditate
Exercise
Gratitude log
Sleep 7+ hours
Connect with others
Avoid alcohol
Less meat
Less dairy
Less refined carbs
Keep notes of triggers
Take Vitamin B12
Take Vitamin D

MY PRIORITIES FOR THIS WEEK

GRATITUDE LOG

MAIN GOALS

DAILY ACTIVITIES

	M	T	W	T	F	S	S
Meditate	○	○	○	○	○	○	○
Exercise	○	○	○	○	○	○	○
Gratitude log	○	○	○	○	○	○	○
Sleep 7+ hours	○	○	○	○	○	○	○
Connect with others	○	○	○	○	○	○	○
Avoid alcohol	○	○	○	○	○	○	○
Less meat	○	○	○	○	○	○	○
Less dairy	○	○	○	○	○	○	○
Less refined carbs	○	○	○	○	○	○	○
Keep notes of triggers	○	○	○	○	○	○	○
Take Vitamin B12	○	○	○	○	○	○	○
Take Vitamin D	○	○	○	○	○	○	○

MY PRIORITIES FOR THIS WEEK

GRATITUDE LOG

MAIN GOALS

DAILY ACTIVITIES

	M	T	W	T	F	S	S
Meditate	○	○	○	○	○	○	○
Exercise	○	○	○	○	○	○	○
Gratitude log	○	○	○	○	○	○	○
Sleep 7+ hours	○	○	○	○	○	○	○
Connect with others	○	○	○	○	○	○	○
Avoid alcohol	○	○	○	○	○	○	○
Less meat	○	○	○	○	○	○	○
Less dairy	○	○	○	○	○	○	○
Less refined carbs	○	○	○	○	○	○	○
Keep notes of triggers	○	○	○	○	○	○	○
Take Vitamin B12	○	○	○	○	○	○	○
Take Vitamin D	○	○	○	○	○	○	○

WEEK OF:

MY PRIORITIES FOR THIS WEEK

GRATITUDE LOG

MAIN GOALS

DAILY ACTIVITIES

M T W T F S S

Meditate
Exercise
Gratitude log
Sleep 7+ hours
Connect with others
Avoid alcohol
Less meat
Less dairy
Less refined carbs
Keep notes of
triggers
Take Vitamin B12
Take Vitamin D

WEEK OF:

MY PRIORITIES FOR THIS WEEK

GRATITUDE LOG

MAIN GOALS

DAILY ACTIVITIES

M T W T F S S

Meditate
Exercise
Gratitude log
Sleep 7+ hours
Connect with others
Avoid alcohol
Less meat
Less dairy
Less refined carbs
Keep notes of triggers
Take Vitamin B12
Take Vitamin D

MY PRIORITIES FOR THIS WEEK

GRATITUDE LOG

MAIN GOALS

DAILY ACTIVITIES

	M	T	W	T	F	S	S
Meditate	○	○	○	○	○	○	○
Exercise	○	○	○	○	○	○	○
Gratitude log	○	○	○	○	○	○	○
Sleep 7+ hours	○	○	○	○	○	○	○
Connect with others	○	○	○	○	○	○	○
Avoid alcohol	○	○	○	○	○	○	○
Less meat	○	○	○	○	○	○	○
Less dairy	○	○	○	○	○	○	○
Less refined carbs	○	○	○	○	○	○	○
Keep notes of triggers	○	○	○	○	○	○	○
Take Vitamin B12	○	○	○	○	○	○	○
Take Vitamin D	○	○	○	○	○	○	○

MY PRIORITIES FOR THIS WEEK

GRATITUDE LOG

MAIN GOALS

DAILY ACTIVITIES

	M	T	W	T	F	S	S
Meditate	○	○	○	○	○	○	○
Exercise	○	○	○	○	○	○	○
Gratitude log	○	○	○	○	○	○	○
Sleep 7+ hours	○	○	○	○	○	○	○
Connect with others	○	○	○	○	○	○	○
Avoid alcohol	○	○	○	○	○	○	○
Less meat	○	○	○	○	○	○	○
Less dairy	○	○	○	○	○	○	○
Less refined carbs	○	○	○	○	○	○	○
Keep notes of triggers	○	○	○	○	○	○	○
Take Vitamin B12	○	○	○	○	○	○	○
Take Vitamin D	○	○	○	○	○	○	○

MY PRIORITIES FOR THIS WEEK

GRATITUDE LOG

MAIN GOALS

DAILY ACTIVITIES

	M	T	W	T	F	S	S
Meditate	○	○	○	○	○	○	○
Exercise	○	○	○	○	○	○	○
Gratitude log	○	○	○	○	○	○	○
Sleep 7+ hours	○	○	○	○	○	○	○
Connect with others	○	○	○	○	○	○	○
Avoid alcohol	○	○	○	○	○	○	○
Less meat	○	○	○	○	○	○	○
Less dairy	○	○	○	○	○	○	○
Less refined carbs	○	○	○	○	○	○	○
Keep notes of triggers	○	○	○	○	○	○	○
Take Vitamin B12	○	○	○	○	○	○	○
Take Vitamin D	○	○	○	○	○	○	○

MY PRIORITIES FOR THIS WEEK

GRATITUDE LOG

MAIN GOALS

DAILY ACTIVITIES

	M	T	W	T	F	S	S
Meditate	○	○	○	○	○	○	○
Exercise	○	○	○	○	○	○	○
Gratitude log	○	○	○	○	○	○	○
Sleep 7+ hours	○	○	○	○	○	○	○
Connect with others	○	○	○	○	○	○	○
Avoid alcohol	○	○	○	○	○	○	○
Less meat	○	○	○	○	○	○	○
Less dairy	○	○	○	○	○	○	○
Less refined carbs	○	○	○	○	○	○	○
Keep notes of triggers	○	○	○	○	○	○	○
Take Vitamin B12	○	○	○	○	○	○	○
Take Vitamin D	○	○	○	○	○	○	○

WEEK OF:

MY PRIORITIES FOR THIS WEEK

GRATITUDE LOG

MAIN GOALS

DAILY ACTIVITIES

	M	T	W	T	F	S	S
Meditate	◯	◯	◯	◯	◯	◯	◯
Exercise	◯	◯	◯	◯	◯	◯	◯
Gratitude log	◯	◯	◯	◯	◯	◯	◯
Sleep 7+ hours	◯	◯	◯	◯	◯	◯	◯
Connect with others	◯	◯	◯	◯	◯	◯	◯
Avoid alcohol	◯	◯	◯	◯	◯	◯	◯
Less meat	◯	◯	◯	◯	◯	◯	◯
Less dairy	◯	◯	◯	◯	◯	◯	◯
Less refined carbs	◯	◯	◯	◯	◯	◯	◯
Keep notes of triggers	◯	◯	◯	◯	◯	◯	◯
Take Vitamin B12	◯	◯	◯	◯	◯	◯	◯
Take Vitamin D	◯	◯	◯	◯	◯	◯	◯

MY PRIORITIES FOR THIS WEEK

GRATITUDE LOG

MAIN GOALS

DAILY ACTIVITIES

	M	T	W	T	F	S	S
Meditate	○	○	○	○	○	○	○
Exercise	○	○	○	○	○	○	○
Gratitude log	○	○	○	○	○	○	○
Sleep 7+ hours	○	○	○	○	○	○	○
Connect with others	○	○	○	○	○	○	○
Avoid alcohol	○	○	○	○	○	○	○
Less meat	○	○	○	○	○	○	○
Less dairy	○	○	○	○	○	○	○
Less refined carbs	○	○	○	○	○	○	○
Keep notes of triggers	○	○	○	○	○	○	○
Take Vitamin B12	○	○	○	○	○	○	○
Take Vitamin D	○	○	○	○	○	○	○

MY PRIORITIES FOR THIS WEEK

GRATITUDE LOG

MAIN GOALS

DAILY ACTIVITIES

	M	T	W	T	F	S	S
Meditate	○	○	○	○	○	○	○
Exercise	○	○	○	○	○	○	○
Gratitude log	○	○	○	○	○	○	○
Sleep 7+ hours	○	○	○	○	○	○	○
Connect with others	○	○	○	○	○	○	○
Avoid alcohol	○	○	○	○	○	○	○
Less meat	○	○	○	○	○	○	○
Less dairy	○	○	○	○	○	○	○
Less refined carbs	○	○	○	○	○	○	○
Keep notes of triggers	○	○	○	○	○	○	○
Take Vitamin B12	○	○	○	○	○	○	○
Take Vitamin D	○	○	○	○	○	○	○

MY PRIORITIES FOR THIS WEEK

GRATITUDE LOG

MAIN GOALS

DAILY ACTIVITIES

	M	T	W	T	F	S	S
Meditate	○	○	○	○	○	○	○
Exercise	○	○	○	○	○	○	○
Gratitude log	○	○	○	○	○	○	○
Sleep 7+ hours	○	○	○	○	○	○	○
Connect with others	○	○	○	○	○	○	○
Avoid alcohol	○	○	○	○	○	○	○
Less meat	○	○	○	○	○	○	○
Less dairy	○	○	○	○	○	○	○
Less refined carbs	○	○	○	○	○	○	○
Keep notes of triggers	○	○	○	○	○	○	○
Take Vitamin B12	○	○	○	○	○	○	○
Take Vitamin D	○	○	○	○	○	○	○

MY PRIORITIES FOR THIS WEEK

GRATITUDE LOG

MAIN GOALS

DAILY ACTIVITIES

	M	T	W	T	F	S	S
Meditate	○	○	○	○	○	○	○
Exercise	○	○	○	○	○	○	○
Gratitude log	○	○	○	○	○	○	○
Sleep 7+ hours	○	○	○	○	○	○	○
Connect with others	○	○	○	○	○	○	○
Avoid alcohol	○	○	○	○	○	○	○
Less meat	○	○	○	○	○	○	○
Less dairy	○	○	○	○	○	○	○
Less refined carbs	○	○	○	○	○	○	○
Keep notes of triggers	○	○	○	○	○	○	○
Take Vitamin B12	○	○	○	○	○	○	○
Take Vitamin D	○	○	○	○	○	○	○

WEEK OF:

MY PRIORITIES FOR THIS WEEK

GRATITUDE LOG

MAIN GOALS

DAILY ACTIVITIES

M T W T F S S

Meditate
Exercise
Gratitude log
Sleep 7+ hours
Connect with others
Avoid alcohol
Less meat
Less dairy
Less refined carbs
Keep notes of triggers
Take Vitamin B12
Take Vitamin D

MY PRIORITIES FOR THIS WEEK

GRATITUDE LOG

MAIN GOALS

DAILY ACTIVITIES

	M	T	W	T	F	S	S
Meditate	○	○	○	○	○	○	○
Exercise	○	○	○	○	○	○	○
Gratitude log	○	○	○	○	○	○	○
Sleep 7+ hours	○	○	○	○	○	○	○
Connect with others	○	○	○	○	○	○	○
Avoid alcohol	○	○	○	○	○	○	○
Less meat	○	○	○	○	○	○	○
Less dairy	○	○	○	○	○	○	○
Less refined carbs	○	○	○	○	○	○	○
Keep notes of triggers	○	○	○	○	○	○	○
Take Vitamin B12	○	○	○	○	○	○	○
Take Vitamin D	○	○	○	○	○	○	○

MY PRIORITIES FOR THIS WEEK

GRATITUDE LOG

MAIN GOALS

DAILY ACTIVITIES

	M	T	W	T	F	S	S
Meditate	○	○	○	○	○	○	○
Exercise	○	○	○	○	○	○	○
Gratitude log	○	○	○	○	○	○	○
Sleep 7+ hours	○	○	○	○	○	○	○
Connect with others	○	○	○	○	○	○	○
Avoid alcohol	○	○	○	○	○	○	○
Less meat	○	○	○	○	○	○	○
Less dairy	○	○	○	○	○	○	○
Less refined carbs	○	○	○	○	○	○	○
Keep notes of triggers	○	○	○	○	○	○	○
Take Vitamin B12	○	○	○	○	○	○	○
Take Vitamin D	○	○	○	○	○	○	○

MY PRIORITIES FOR THIS WEEK

GRATITUDE LOG

MAIN GOALS

DAILY ACTIVITIES

	M	T	W	T	F	S	S
Meditate	○	○	○	○	○	○	○
Exercise	○	○	○	○	○	○	○
Gratitude log	○	○	○	○	○	○	○
Sleep 7+ hours	○	○	○	○	○	○	○
Connect with others	○	○	○	○	○	○	○
Avoid alcohol	○	○	○	○	○	○	○
Less meat	○	○	○	○	○	○	○
Less dairy	○	○	○	○	○	○	○
Less refined carbs	○	○	○	○	○	○	○
Keep notes of triggers	○	○	○	○	○	○	○
Take Vitamin B12	○	○	○	○	○	○	○
Take Vitamin D	○	○	○	○	○	○	○

MY PRIORITIES FOR THIS WEEK

GRATITUDE LOG

MAIN GOALS

DAILY ACTIVITIES

	M	T	W	T	F	S	S
Meditate	○	○	○	○	○	○	○
Exercise	○	○	○	○	○	○	○
Gratitude log	○	○	○	○	○	○	○
Sleep 7+ hours	○	○	○	○	○	○	○
Connect with others	○	○	○	○	○	○	○
Avoid alcohol	○	○	○	○	○	○	○
Less meat	○	○	○	○	○	○	○
Less dairy	○	○	○	○	○	○	○
Less refined carbs	○	○	○	○	○	○	○
Keep notes of triggers	○	○	○	○	○	○	○
Take Vitamin B12	○	○	○	○	○	○	○
Take Vitamin D	○	○	○	○	○	○	○

MY PRIORITIES FOR THIS WEEK

GRATITUDE LOG

MAIN GOALS

DAILY ACTIVITIES

	M	T	W	T	F	S	S
Meditate	○	○	○	○	○	○	○
Exercise	○	○	○	○	○	○	○
Gratitude log	○	○	○	○	○	○	○
Sleep 7+ hours	○	○	○	○	○	○	○
Connect with others	○	○	○	○	○	○	○
Avoid alcohol	○	○	○	○	○	○	○
Less meat	○	○	○	○	○	○	○
Less dairy	○	○	○	○	○	○	○
Less refined carbs	○	○	○	○	○	○	○
Keep notes of triggers	○	○	○	○	○	○	○
Take Vitamin B12	○	○	○	○	○	○	○
Take Vitamin D	○	○	○	○	○	○	○

WEEK OF:

MY PRIORITIES FOR THIS WEEK

GRATITUDE LOG

MAIN GOALS

DAILY ACTIVITIES

M T W T F S S

Meditate
Exercise
Gratitude log
Sleep 7+ hours
Connect with others
Avoid alcohol
Less meat
Less dairy
Less refined carbs
Keep notes of triggers
Take Vitamin B12
Take Vitamin D

MY PRIORITIES FOR THIS WEEK

GRATITUDE LOG

MAIN GOALS

DAILY ACTIVITIES

	M	T	W	T	F	S	S
Meditate	○	○	○	○	○	○	○
Exercise	○	○	○	○	○	○	○
Gratitude log	○	○	○	○	○	○	○
Sleep 7+ hours	○	○	○	○	○	○	○
Connect with others	○	○	○	○	○	○	○
Avoid alcohol	○	○	○	○	○	○	○
Less meat	○	○	○	○	○	○	○
Less dairy	○	○	○	○	○	○	○
Less refined carbs	○	○	○	○	○	○	○
Keep notes of triggers	○	○	○	○	○	○	○
Take Vitamin B12	○	○	○	○	○	○	○
Take Vitamin D	○	○	○	○	○	○	○

MY PRIORITIES FOR THIS WEEK

GRATITUDE LOG

MAIN GOALS

DAILY ACTIVITIES

	M	T	W	T	F	S	S
Meditate	○	○	○	○	○	○	○
Exercise	○	○	○	○	○	○	○
Gratitude log	○	○	○	○	○	○	○
Sleep 7+ hours	○	○	○	○	○	○	○
Connect with others	○	○	○	○	○	○	○
Avoid alcohol	○	○	○	○	○	○	○
Less meat	○	○	○	○	○	○	○
Less dairy	○	○	○	○	○	○	○
Less refined carbs	○	○	○	○	○	○	○
Keep notes of triggers	○	○	○	○	○	○	○
Take Vitamin B12	○	○	○	○	○	○	○
Take Vitamin D	○	○	○	○	○	○	○

MY PRIORITIES FOR THIS WEEK

GRATITUDE LOG

MAIN GOALS

DAILY ACTIVITIES

	M	T	W	T	F	S	S
Meditate	○	○	○	○	○	○	○
Exercise	○	○	○	○	○	○	○
Gratitude log	○	○	○	○	○	○	○
Sleep 7+ hours	○	○	○	○	○	○	○
Connect with others	○	○	○	○	○	○	○
Avoid alcohol	○	○	○	○	○	○	○
Less meat	○	○	○	○	○	○	○
Less dairy	○	○	○	○	○	○	○
Less refined carbs	○	○	○	○	○	○	○
Keep notes of triggers	○	○	○	○	○	○	○
Take Vitamin B12	○	○	○	○	○	○	○
Take Vitamin D	○	○	○	○	○	○	○

MY PRIORITIES FOR THIS WEEK

GRATITUDE LOG

MAIN GOALS

DAILY ACTIVITIES

	M	T	W	T	F	S	S
Meditate	○	○	○	○	○	○	○
Exercise	○	○	○	○	○	○	○
Gratitude log	○	○	○	○	○	○	○
Sleep 7+ hours	○	○	○	○	○	○	○
Connect with others	○	○	○	○	○	○	○
Avoid alcohol	○	○	○	○	○	○	○
Less meat	○	○	○	○	○	○	○
Less dairy	○	○	○	○	○	○	○
Less refined carbs	○	○	○	○	○	○	○
Keep notes of triggers	○	○	○	○	○	○	○
Take Vitamin B12	○	○	○	○	○	○	○
Take Vitamin D	○	○	○	○	○	○	○

MY PRIORITIES FOR THIS WEEK

GRATITUDE LOG

MAIN GOALS

DAILY ACTIVITIES

	M	T	W	T	F	S	S
Meditate	○	○	○	○	○	○	○
Exercise	○	○	○	○	○	○	○
Gratitude log	○	○	○	○	○	○	○
Sleep 7+ hours	○	○	○	○	○	○	○
Connect with others	○	○	○	○	○	○	○
Avoid alcohol	○	○	○	○	○	○	○
Less meat	○	○	○	○	○	○	○
Less dairy	○	○	○	○	○	○	○
Less refined carbs	○	○	○	○	○	○	○
Keep notes of triggers	○	○	○	○	○	○	○
Take Vitamin B12	○	○	○	○	○	○	○
Take Vitamin D	○	○	○	○	○	○	○

MY PRIORITIES FOR THIS WEEK

GRATITUDE LOG

MAIN GOALS

DAILY ACTIVITIES

	M	T	W	T	F	S	S
Meditate	○	○	○	○	○	○	○
Exercise	○	○	○	○	○	○	○
Gratitude log	○	○	○	○	○	○	○
Sleep 7+ hours	○	○	○	○	○	○	○
Connect with others	○	○	○	○	○	○	○
Avoid alcohol	○	○	○	○	○	○	○
Less meat	○	○	○	○	○	○	○
Less dairy	○	○	○	○	○	○	○
Less refined carbs	○	○	○	○	○	○	○
Keep notes of triggers	○	○	○	○	○	○	○
Take Vitamin B12	○	○	○	○	○	○	○
Take Vitamin D	○	○	○	○	○	○	○

MY PRIORITIES FOR THIS WEEK

GRATITUDE LOG

MAIN GOALS

DAILY ACTIVITIES

	M	T	W	T	F	S	S
Meditate	○	○	○	○	○	○	○
Exercise	○	○	○	○	○	○	○
Gratitude log	○	○	○	○	○	○	○
Sleep 7+ hours	○	○	○	○	○	○	○
Connect with others	○	○	○	○	○	○	○
Avoid alcohol	○	○	○	○	○	○	○
Less meat	○	○	○	○	○	○	○
Less dairy	○	○	○	○	○	○	○
Less refined carbs	○	○	○	○	○	○	○
Keep notes of triggers	○	○	○	○	○	○	○
Take Vitamin B12	○	○	○	○	○	○	○
Take Vitamin D	○	○	○	○	○	○	○

MY PRIORITIES FOR THIS WEEK

GRATITUDE LOG

MAIN GOALS

DAILY ACTIVITIES

	M	T	W	T	F	S	S
Meditate	○	○	○	○	○	○	○
Exercise	○	○	○	○	○	○	○
Gratitude log	○	○	○	○	○	○	○
Sleep 7+ hours	○	○	○	○	○	○	○
Connect with others	○	○	○	○	○	○	○
Avoid alcohol	○	○	○	○	○	○	○
Less meat	○	○	○	○	○	○	○
Less dairy	○	○	○	○	○	○	○
Less refined carbs	○	○	○	○	○	○	○
Keep notes of triggers	○	○	○	○	○	○	○
Take Vitamin B12	○	○	○	○	○	○	○
Take Vitamin D	○	○	○	○	○	○	○

MY PRIORITIES FOR THIS WEEK

GRATITUDE LOG

MAIN GOALS

DAILY ACTIVITIES

	M	T	W	T	F	S	S
Meditate	○	○	○	○	○	○	○
Exercise	○	○	○	○	○	○	○
Gratitude log	○	○	○	○	○	○	○
Sleep 7+ hours	○	○	○	○	○	○	○
Connect with others	○	○	○	○	○	○	○
Avoid alcohol	○	○	○	○	○	○	○
Less meat	○	○	○	○	○	○	○
Less dairy	○	○	○	○	○	○	○
Less refined carbs	○	○	○	○	○	○	○
Keep notes of triggers	○	○	○	○	○	○	○
Take Vitamin B12	○	○	○	○	○	○	○
Take Vitamin D	○	○	○	○	○	○	○

	M	T	W	T	F	S	S
Meditate	○	○	○	○	○	○	○
Exercise	○	○	○	○	○	○	○
Gratitude log	○	○	○	○	○	○	○
Sleep 7+ hours	○	○	○	○	○	○	○
Connect with others	○	○	○	○	○	○	○
Avoid alcohol	○	○	○	○	○	○	○
Less meat	○	○	○	○	○	○	○
Less dairy	○	○	○	○	○	○	○
Less refined carbs	○	○	○	○	○	○	○
Keep notes of triggers	○	○	○	○	○	○	○
Take Vitamin B12	○	○	○	○	○	○	○
Take Vitamin D	○	○	○	○	○	○	○

MY PRIORITIES FOR THIS WEEK

GRATITUDE LOG

MAIN GOALS

DAILY ACTIVITIES

	M	T	W	T	F	S	S
Meditate	○	○	○	○	○	○	○
Exercise	○	○	○	○	○	○	○
Gratitude log	○	○	○	○	○	○	○
Sleep 7+ hours	○	○	○	○	○	○	○
Connect with others	○	○	○	○	○	○	○
Avoid alcohol	○	○	○	○	○	○	○
Less meat	○	○	○	○	○	○	○
Less dairy	○	○	○	○	○	○	○
Less refined carbs	○	○	○	○	○	○	○
Keep notes of triggers	○	○	○	○	○	○	○
Take Vitamin B12	○	○	○	○	○	○	○
Take Vitamin D	○	○	○	○	○	○	○

MY PRIORITIES FOR THIS WEEK

GRATITUDE LOG

MAIN GOALS

DAILY ACTIVITIES

	M	T	W	T	F	S	S
Meditate	○	○	○	○	○	○	○
Exercise	○	○	○	○	○	○	○
Gratitude log	○	○	○	○	○	○	○
Sleep 7+ hours	○	○	○	○	○	○	○
Connect with others	○	○	○	○	○	○	○
Avoid alcohol	○	○	○	○	○	○	○
Less meat	○	○	○	○	○	○	○
Less dairy	○	○	○	○	○	○	○
Less refined carbs	○	○	○	○	○	○	○
Keep notes of triggers	○	○	○	○	○	○	○
Take Vitamin B12	○	○	○	○	○	○	○
Take Vitamin D	○	○	○	○	○	○	○

MY PRIORITIES FOR THIS WEEK

GRATITUDE LOG

MAIN GOALS

DAILY ACTIVITIES

	M	T	W	T	F	S	S
Meditate	○	○	○	○	○	○	○
Exercise	○	○	○	○	○	○	○
Gratitude log	○	○	○	○	○	○	○
Sleep 7+ hours	○	○	○	○	○	○	○
Connect with others	○	○	○	○	○	○	○
Avoid alcohol	○	○	○	○	○	○	○
Less meat	○	○	○	○	○	○	○
Less dairy	○	○	○	○	○	○	○
Less refined carbs	○	○	○	○	○	○	○
Keep notes of triggers	○	○	○	○	○	○	○
Take Vitamin B12	○	○	○	○	○	○	○
Take Vitamin D	○	○	○	○	○	○	○

MY PRIORITIES FOR THIS WEEK

GRATITUDE LOG

MAIN GOALS

DAILY ACTIVITIES

	M	T	W	T	F	S	S
Meditate							
Exercise							
Gratitude log							
Sleep 7+ hours							
Connect with others							
Avoid alcohol							
Less meat							
Less dairy							
Less refined carbs							
Keep notes of triggers							
Take Vitamin B12							
Take Vitamin D							

MY PRIORITIES FOR THIS WEEK

GRATITUDE LOG

MAIN GOALS

DAILY ACTIVITIES

	M	T	W	T	F	S	S
Meditate	○	○	○	○	○	○	○
Exercise	○	○	○	○	○	○	○
Gratitude log	○	○	○	○	○	○	○
Sleep 7+ hours	○	○	○	○	○	○	○
Connect with others	○	○	○	○	○	○	○
Avoid alcohol	○	○	○	○	○	○	○
Less meat	○	○	○	○	○	○	○
Less dairy	○	○	○	○	○	○	○
Less refined carbs	○	○	○	○	○	○	○
Keep notes of triggers	○	○	○	○	○	○	○
Take Vitamin B12	○	○	○	○	○	○	○
Take Vitamin D	○	○	○	○	○	○	○

MY PRIORITIES FOR THIS WEEK

GRATITUDE LOG

MAIN GOALS

DAILY ACTIVITIES

	M	T	W	T	F	S	S
Meditate	◯	◯	◯	◯	◯	◯	◯
Exercise	◯	◯	◯	◯	◯	◯	◯
Gratitude log	◯	◯	◯	◯	◯	◯	◯
Sleep 7+ hours	◯	◯	◯	◯	◯	◯	◯
Connect with others	◯	◯	◯	◯	◯	◯	◯
Avoid alcohol	◯	◯	◯	◯	◯	◯	◯
Less meat	◯	◯	◯	◯	◯	◯	◯
Less dairy	◯	◯	◯	◯	◯	◯	◯
Less refined carbs	◯	◯	◯	◯	◯	◯	◯
Keep notes of triggers	◯	◯	◯	◯	◯	◯	◯
Take Vitamin B12	◯	◯	◯	◯	◯	◯	◯
Take Vitamin D	◯	◯	◯	◯	◯	◯	◯

MY PRIORITIES FOR THIS WEEK

GRATITUDE LOG

MAIN GOALS

DAILY ACTIVITIES

	M	T	W	T	F	S	S
Meditate	○	○	○	○	○	○	○
Exercise	○	○	○	○	○	○	○
Gratitude log	○	○	○	○	○	○	○
Sleep 7+ hours	○	○	○	○	○	○	○
Connect with others	○	○	○	○	○	○	○
Avoid alcohol	○	○	○	○	○	○	○
Less meat	○	○	○	○	○	○	○
Less dairy	○	○	○	○	○	○	○
Less refined carbs	○	○	○	○	○	○	○
Keep notes of triggers	○	○	○	○	○	○	○
Take Vitamin B12	○	○	○	○	○	○	○
Take Vitamin D	○	○	○	○	○	○	○

MY PRIORITIES FOR THIS WEEK

GRATITUDE LOG

MAIN GOALS

DAILY ACTIVITIES

	M	T	W	T	F	S	S
Meditate	○	○	○	○	○	○	○
Exercise	○	○	○	○	○	○	○
Gratitude log	○	○	○	○	○	○	○
Sleep 7+ hours	○	○	○	○	○	○	○
Connect with others	○	○	○	○	○	○	○
Avoid alcohol	○	○	○	○	○	○	○
Less meat	○	○	○	○	○	○	○
Less dairy	○	○	○	○	○	○	○
Less refined carbs	○	○	○	○	○	○	○
Keep notes of triggers	○	○	○	○	○	○	○
Take Vitamin B12	○	○	○	○	○	○	○
Take Vitamin D	○	○	○	○	○	○	○

MY PRIORITIES FOR THIS WEEK

GRATITUDE LOG

MAIN GOALS

DAILY ACTIVITIES

	M	T	W	T	F	S	S
Meditate	○	○	○	○	○	○	○
Exercise	○	○	○	○	○	○	○
Gratitude log	○	○	○	○	○	○	○
Sleep 7+ hours	○	○	○	○	○	○	○
Connect with others	○	○	○	○	○	○	○
Avoid alcohol	○	○	○	○	○	○	○
Less meat	○	○	○	○	○	○	○
Less dairy	○	○	○	○	○	○	○
Less refined carbs	○	○	○	○	○	○	○
Keep notes of triggers	○	○	○	○	○	○	○
Take Vitamin B12	○	○	○	○	○	○	○
Take Vitamin D	○	○	○	○	○	○	○

MY PRIORITIES FOR THIS WEEK

GRATITUDE LOG

MAIN GOALS

DAILY ACTIVITIES

	M	T	W	T	F	S	S
Meditate	○	○	○	○	○	○	○
Exercise	○	○	○	○	○	○	○
Gratitude log	○	○	○	○	○	○	○
Sleep 7+ hours	○	○	○	○	○	○	○
Connect with others	○	○	○	○	○	○	○
Avoid alcohol	○	○	○	○	○	○	○
Less meat	○	○	○	○	○	○	○
Less dairy	○	○	○	○	○	○	○
Less refined carbs	○	○	○	○	○	○	○
Keep notes of triggers	○	○	○	○	○	○	○
Take Vitamin B12	○	○	○	○	○	○	○
Take Vitamin D	○	○	○	○	○	○	○

MY PRIORITIES FOR THIS WEEK

GRATITUDE LOG

MAIN GOALS

DAILY ACTIVITIES

	M	T	W	T	F	S	S
Meditate	○	○	○	○	○	○	○
Exercise	○	○	○	○	○	○	○
Gratitude log	○	○	○	○	○	○	○
Sleep 7+ hours	○	○	○	○	○	○	○
Connect with others	○	○	○	○	○	○	○
Avoid alcohol	○	○	○	○	○	○	○
Less meat	○	○	○	○	○	○	○
Less dairy	○	○	○	○	○	○	○
Less refined carbs	○	○	○	○	○	○	○
Keep notes of triggers	○	○	○	○	○	○	○
Take Vitamin B12	○	○	○	○	○	○	○
Take Vitamin D	○	○	○	○	○	○	○

MY PRIORITIES FOR THIS WEEK

GRATITUDE LOG

MAIN GOALS

DAILY ACTIVITIES

	M	T	W	T	F	S	S
Meditate	○	○	○	○	○	○	○
Exercise	○	○	○	○	○	○	○
Gratitude log	○	○	○	○	○	○	○
Sleep 7+ hours	○	○	○	○	○	○	○
Connect with others	○	○	○	○	○	○	○
Avoid alcohol	○	○	○	○	○	○	○
Less meat	○	○	○	○	○	○	○
Less dairy	○	○	○	○	○	○	○
Less refined carbs	○	○	○	○	○	○	○
Keep notes of triggers	○	○	○	○	○	○	○
Take Vitamin B12	○	○	○	○	○	○	○
Take Vitamin D	○	○	○	○	○	○	○

MY PRIORITIES FOR THIS WEEK

GRATITUDE LOG

MAIN GOALS

DAILY ACTIVITIES

	M	T	W	T	F	S	S
Meditate	○	○	○	○	○	○	○
Exercise	○	○	○	○	○	○	○
Gratitude log	○	○	○	○	○	○	○
Sleep 7+ hours	○	○	○	○	○	○	○
Connect with others	○	○	○	○	○	○	○
Avoid alcohol	○	○	○	○	○	○	○
Less meat	○	○	○	○	○	○	○
Less dairy	○	○	○	○	○	○	○
Less refined carbs	○	○	○	○	○	○	○
Keep notes of triggers	○	○	○	○	○	○	○
Take Vitamin B12	○	○	○	○	○	○	○
Take Vitamin D	○	○	○	○	○	○	○